Brexit and th
of the European Union

Brexit and the Future of the European Union

The Case for Constitutional Reforms

FEDERICO FABBRINI

OXFORD
UNIVERSITY PRESS

Great Clarendon Street, Oxford, OX2 6DP,
United Kingdom

Oxford University Press is a department of the University of Oxford.
It furthers the University's objective of excellence in research, scholarship,
and education by publishing worldwide. Oxford is a registered trade mark of
Oxford University Press in the UK and in certain other countries

First Edition published in 2020

Impression: 4

Published in the United States of America by Oxford University Press
198 Madison Avenue, New York, NY 10016, United States of America

British Library Cataloguing in Publication Data

Data available

Library of Congress Control Number: 2020942703

ISBN 978-0-19-887126-2 (hbk.)
ISBN 978-0-19-887127-9 (pbk.)

DOI: 10.1093/oso/9780198871262.001.0001

Printed and bound by
CPI Group (UK) Ltd, Croydon, CR0 4YY

Acknowledgements

I deliver this book as part of the Charlemagne Prize fellowship I was awarded by the Karlspreis Stiftung, in Aachen, Germany in November 2019. My sincere thanks go to the Charlemagne Prize Academy, and particularly Jürgen Linden (Chairman of the Board of Directors of the Charlemagne Prize Society) and Christine Klemm (Coordinator of the Charlemagne Prize Academy), for supporting my research on the Conference on the Future of Europe.

The work behind this book is four years in the making. Since winning a chair in Law at the School of Law & Government of Dublin City University in June 2016—ironically on the day of the Brexit referendum—I have been interested in exploring the implications that the withdrawal of the United Kingdom from the European Union has for the future of Europe. Moreover, my research on this topic has intensified since 2017, when I established the Brexit Institute, which I direct. This book brings together my thoughts on what Brexit means for the EU. As such, this book is not about Brexit per se—which is thoroughly covered in the book series *The Law & Politics of Brexit* I edit at Oxford University Press. Rather, it focuses on the future of the EU, and makes the case for reforms, suggesting that Brexit is such a momentous development that it cannot be minimized, or let pass, without an adequate renewal of the European project.

The book develops and expands earlier ideas and materials, including: 'The Future of the EU27' (2019) Special Issue *European Journal of Legal Studies* 305; 'The Composition of the European Parliament in Brexit Times: Changes and Challenges' (2019) 44 *European Law Review* 711, with Rebecca Schmidt; and 'The Conference on the Future of Europe: A New Model to Reform the EU', Charlemagne Prize & Brexit Institute working paper n° 12/2019. Moreover, it defends views I first outlined in three studies I was commissioned to write by the European Parliament Constitutional Affairs (AFCO) Committee: 'The Institutional Consequences of a "Hard Brexit"' (May 2018); 'A Fiscal Capacity for the

Eurozone: Constitutional Perspectives' (February 2019); and 'Possible Avenues for Further Political Integration in Europe' (May 2020).

I want to thank Giuliano Amato and Sergio Fabbrini for sharing their thoughts on a first draft of this manuscript and for their own cutting-edge research and policy on Europe's future.

This book on the future of Europe is dedicated with love to Silvia, for our past, present—and future together.

23 June 2020

Contents

Table of Cases

Short Bio

Federico Fabbrini (Trento, 1985) is Full Professor of EU Law at the School of Law & Government of Dublin City University (DCU), where he is also the founding Director of the Brexit Institute and the principal investigator of the EU-funded Jean Monnet Network on the future of Europe entitled BRIDGE ('Brexit Research and Interchange on Differentiated Governance in Europe'—project n. 611710-EPP-1-2019-1-IE-EPPJMO-NETWORK).

Federico Fabbrini holds a PhD in Law from the European University Institute and previously held academic positions in the Netherlands and Denmark. He is the author of over 100 scientific publications, including *Fundamental Rights in Europe* (Oxford University Press 2014), *Economic Governance in Europe* (Oxford University Press 2016), and *Introduzione al diritto dell'Unione europea* (Il Mulino 2018). Moreover, he is the editor of several collective volumes and special journal issues, including *The Law & Politics of Brexit* (Oxford University Press 2017), and *The Law & Politics of Brexit. Volume II. The Withdrawal Agreement* (Oxford University Press 2020—with a Foreword by Michel Barnier).

He regularly engages with the EU institutions and on three occasions he was requested to write reports for the European Parliament Constitutional Affairs (AFCO) Committee.

In November 2019, he was awarded the Charlemagne Prize fellowship for research for his work on the Conference on the Future of Europe.

List of Abbreviations

AFCO	Committee on Constitutional Affairs
ALDE Party	Alliance of Liberals and Democrats for Europe (ALDE) Party
CAP	Common Agricultural Policy
CCPs	central counterparties
CFSDP	common foreign, security, and defence policy
EBA	European Banking Authority
ECAS	European Common Asylum System
ECB	European Central Bank
ECON Committee	Economic and Monetary Affairs Committee
ECtHR	European Court of Human Rights
ECJ	European Court of Justice
ECR	European Conservatives & Reformists
ECSC	European Carbon and Steel Community
EDC	European Defence Community
EDIS	European deposit insurance scheme
EEC	European Economic Community
EIB	European Investment Bank
EMA	European Medical Agency
EMU	Economic and Monetary Union
EPP	European Peoples' Party
EPPO	European Public Prosecutor's Office
ESM	European Stability Mechanism
ESMA	European Securities and Markets Authority
EU	European Union
Euratom	European Atomic Energy Community
GDP	gross domestic product
GUE/NGL	European United Left–Nordic Green Left
ID	Identity & Democracy
IGC	intergovernmental conference
MEPs	Members of the European Parliament
MFF	multi-annual financial framework
PESCO	Permanent Structured Cooperation
PSPP	public sector purchase programme
S&D	Socialists & Democrats
SGP	Stability and Growth Pact

SRF	Single Resolution Fund
SSM	Single Supervisory Mechanism
SURE	Support to mitigate Unemployment Risks in an Emergency
TEU	Treaty on European Union
TFEU	Treaty on the Functioning of the European Union
UK	United Kingdom
US	United States

1

Introduction

The withdrawal of the United Kingdom (UK) from the European Union
(EU)—a process colloquially called Brexit—represents a profound shock
for the project of European integration. Since its creation with the Treaty
of Paris of 1951 and the Treaties of Rome in 1957, the EU has been in-
spired by the idea that Member States were committed to a process of
'ever closer Union'.[1] Historical developments seemed to vindicate that
view: in 60 years, EU membership had widened from six to 28 Member
States and EU competences have deepened, increasingly absorbing hallmarks of state sovereignty. The EU gradually tied Member States and
their citizens closer together and succeeded in transforming a continent
of warring states into a *Rechtsgemeinschaft*. However, the referendum of
23 June 2016, where the people of the UK decided by majority to leave the
EU,[2] and the eventual withdrawal of the UK from the EU on 31 January
2020,[3] unsettled the assumptions of the European integration narrative
and raised new questions on the *finalité* of the EU project.

The aim of this book is to analyse the consequences of Brexit for the EU.
As such, the interest here is not on Brexit per se. Indeed, much work already exists on the law and politics of the referendum,[4] the agreement on
the withdrawal of the UK from the EU,[5] and the framework of future EU–
UK relations.[6] Rather, this book seeks to shed light on how the EU has
been affected by the UK's decision to leave—and what this means for the

---

[1] Preamble, TEU.
[2] The UK Electoral Commission, Results and turnout at the EU referendum http://www.
electoralcommission.org.uk/find-information-by-subject/elections-and-referendums/past-
elections-and-referendums/eu-referendum/electorate-and-count-information.
[3] Agreement on the withdrawal of the United Kingdom of Great Britain and Northern Ireland
from the European Union and the European Atomic Energy Community, OJ 2020 L 29/07.
[4] Federico Fabbrini (ed), *The Law & Politics of Brexit* (OUP 2017).
[5] Federico Fabbrini (ed), *The Law & Politics of Brexit: Volume II: The Withdrawal Agreement*
(OUP 2020).
[6] Federico Fabbrini (ed), *The Law & Politics of Brexit: Volume III: The Framework of Future
EU-UK Relations* (OUP 2021).

Brexit and the Future of the European Union. Federico Fabbrini, Oxford University Press (2020). © Federico
Fabbrini. DOI: 10.1093/oso/9780198871262.003.0001

future of European integration. Notwithstanding the tendency in certain circles to minimize the UK's withdrawal from the EU, blaming it on the idiosyncratic British approach to European integration, Brexit cannot be treated as business as usual. The departure of a large, rich, and influential Member State must prompt a rethink of the EU constitutional settlement. In fact, immediately after the Brexit referendum, the EU and its Member States started a debate on the future of Europe—and this process is now moving from rhetoric to reality with the institution of the Conference on the Future of Europe.

The core argument of this book is that the EU must renew itself in order to relaunch the process of European integration following the withdrawal of the UK. While the EU and its Member States remained united vis-à-vis the UK during Brexit, successfully handling the withdrawal negotiations, Brexit still created a host of transitional problems for the EU's functioning and funding. Moreover, in the last decade the EU has faced a plurality of other crises besides Brexit—from the euro-crisis, to the migration crisis, and the rule of law crisis—which have profoundly tested the unity of the Member States and dramatically exposed the shortcomings of the current EU system of governance. In fact, the challenges for the EU have been aggravated after Brexit by the explosion of the coronavirus: this severe acute respiratory syndrome known by its medical acronym Covid-19, has resulted in the largest pandemic the world has experienced at least since the 1918 Spanish influenza[7] and has caused dramatic health and socio-economic costs.

As a consequence, the book makes the case for EU reforms beyond Brexit, arguing that this is the best way to react to the withdrawal of the UK—increasing the EU's effectiveness and legitimacy. To this end, it analyses the initiative to establish a Conference on the Future of Europe, and discusses options to ensure its success. The Conference on the Future of Europe—an idea originally advanced by French President Emmanuel Macron in March 2019, before the European Parliament (EP) elections, in an open letter addressed to all European citizens (written in the 22 official languages of the EU) *pour une renaissance européenne*[8]—has now

---

[7] See World Health Organization Director General Tedros Adhanom Ghebreyesus, remarks, 11 March 2020 (defining Covid-19 as a global pandemic).

[8] French President Emmanuel Macron, Letter, 4 March 2019 https://www.elysee.fr/es/ emmanuel-macron/2019/03/04/pour-une-renaissance-europeenne.fr.

been endorsed by all EU institutions.[9] This initiative has the potential to be a new model to reform the EU, along the lines of illustrious precedents such as the Conference of Messina and the Convention on the Future of Europe. Nevertheless, if the Conference wants to achieve its ambitions it must deal with treaty change. Yet, there are obstacles in the EU treaty amendment procedure. Alternative opportunities for reforming the EU must therefore be considered, and the use of intergovernmental agreements concluded outside the EU legal order in the context of the euro-crisis provides useful lessons.

As the book claims, the establishment of the Conference on the Future of Europe—70 years after the Schuman Declaration, and 10 years after the entry into force of the Lisbon Treaty—is a long overdue step to reflect on the constitutional future of an EU of now 27 Member States. In light of Brexit, there can be no complacency on the status quo, as the state of the union is not strong—despite the positive performance of the EU vis-à-vis the UK in the withdrawal negotiations. From this point of view, the Conference of the Future of Europe can serve as an innovative means to reform the EU, tackling the transitional issues left by the UK's withdrawal and addressing the more structural substantive and institutional weaknesses dramatically exposed by the plurality of other crises the EU recently weathered. In fact, the Conference on the Future of Europe is made all the more urgent by Covid-19, and the exigencies of the EU post-pandemic recovery plan, which will entail important adjustments to the EU structure of powers and responsibilities.

Nevertheless, there is no doubt that the EU treaty amendment procedure, with the requirement to obtain unanimous approval and ratification by all Member States for any treaty change, represents a major peril for the Conference's prospects—as the failure of the European Constitution proves.[10] The problem of state veto is further compounded by the fact that ever more diverse visions of integration

---

[9] See European Parliament resolution of 15 January 2020 on the European Parliament's position on the Conference on the Future of Europe, P9_TA(2020)0010; European Commission Communication, 'Shaping the Conference on the Future of Europe', 22 January 2020, COM(2020) 27 final; European Parliament resolution of 18 June 2020 on the European Parliament's position on the Conference on the Future of Europe, P9_TA(2020)0153; and Council of the EU, 24 June 2020, Doc. 9102/20.

[10] See Nick Barber et al (eds), *The Rise and Fall of the European Constitution* (Hart Publishing 2019).

are coming to the fore among the Member States. In particular, three ideas of what the EU is and ought to be are increasingly competing: a first that sees the EU as a polity, which requires solidarity and a communion of efforts towards a shared destiny; a second that sees the EU as a market, designed to enhance wealth through commerce, but with as limited redistribution as possible; and a third which instead sees the EU as a vehicle to entrench state autocracy, based on national identity and sovereignty claims, but with crucial transnational financial support. In this context, the search for a one-size-fits-all consensus may be illusory.

Therefore, the Conference on the Future of Europe should consider further possible avenues for political integration in Europe, including the option to conclude a new, separate treaty—call it a Political Compact—subject to new rules on its entry into force that do away with the unanimity requirement in favour of super-majority ratification. This option raises novel questions. Yet, the use of intergovernmental agreements with new, less-than-unanimous, entry-into-force rules is now a consolidated practice in the field of Economic and Monetary Union (EMU), which can usefully be followed as a precedent in other areas as well.[11] In fact, channelling the outcome of the Conference on the Future of Europe into a new compact is ultimately a preferable alternative to the risks of paralysis. If Brexit has proven anything, it is precisely that the EU cannot stand still—and reform is the strategy for the future of Europe following the UK's withdrawal from the EU.

The book's original feature is to use Brexit as a lens to analyse the EU and its future. By regarding the UK's withdrawal from the EU as a momentous event, and a watershed in the history of European integration, this work utilizes Brexit as a prism to shed light on the necessity and urgency of constitutional reforms in the EU. As such, the book is structured as follows.

Chapter 2 analyses the EU during Brexit, explaining how the EU institutions and the Member States reacted to the UK's decision to leave the EU, and outlining how they went about it in the course of the withdrawal negotiations. As this chapter underlines, the EU institutions and the Member States managed to adopt a very united stance vis-à-vis a

---

[11] See further Federico Fabbrini, *Economic Governance in Europe* (OUP 2016).

withdrawing state—establishing effective institutional mechanisms and succeeding in imposing their strategic preferences in the negotiations with the UK. Nevertheless, the EU was also absorbed during Brexit by internal preparations to face both the scenario of a 'hard Brexit'—the UK leaving the EU with no deal—and of a 'no Brexit'—with the UK subsequently delaying exit and extending its EU membership. Finally, during Brexit the EU increasingly started working as a union of 27 Member States—the EU27—which in this format opened a debate on the future of Europe and developed new policy initiatives, especially in the field of defence and military cooperation.

Chapter 3 examines the EU because of Brexit, focusing on a number of transitional problems that the withdrawal of the UK from the EU—and its delay owing to subsequent requests to extend EU membership for extra time—posed for the EU's functioning and funding. In particular, the chapter emphasizes the consequences of Brexit for the composition of the 9th EP (2019–2024), and its elections in May 2019, explaining how the participation of the UK in this democratic process had *pro tempore* effects on both the EP's outlook and its electoral outcome. However, the chapter also examines the transitional institutional challenges faced because of Brexit by both the European Commission and the Council of the EU. Moreover, it underlines the implications of Brexit for the EU multi-annual financial framework (MFF), stressing how the UK's withdrawal created a budget gap for the EU, due to the way in which the EU is funded, and how this was due to create challenges in the next MFF negotiations—as indeed happened.

Chapter 4 analyses the EU besides Brexit, shedding light on the many other crises that the EU has recently faced in addition to the withdrawal of the UK. In the last decade the EU has weathered the euro-crisis, the migration crisis, and the rule of law crisis—each of which has continued to sour throughout the Brexit negotiations. Moreover, on top of these old crises, the EU has now faced new ones—as shown by the difficulties of dealing with the issue of enlargement, the problem of climate change, and particularly the catastrophic Covid-19 pandemic. All these crises have exposed the disunity of the EU—a counter-point to the unity that emerged in the Brexit negotiations. The chapter explains the difficulties of the EU27 in successfully tackling once and for all any of these crises, and the growing centripetal forces at play, owing to the rise of very different visions of European integration—what I call a 'polity', a 'market', and an 'autocracy' conception of the EU, which are competing with each other.

Chapter 5 focuses on the EU after Brexit and articulates the case for constitutional reforms. Reforms are necessary to address the substantive and institutional shortcomings that have patently emerged in the context of Europe's old and new crises. Moreover, reforms will be compelled by the exigencies of the post-Covid-19 EU recovery, which pushes the EU towards new horizons in terms of fiscal federalism and democratic governance. As a result, the chapter considers both obstacles and opportunities to reform the EU and make it more effective and legitimate. On the one hand, it underlines the difficulties connected with the EU treaty amendment procedure, owing to the requirement of unanimous approval of any treaty change, and the consequential problem of the veto. On the other hand, it emphasizes the increasing practice by Member States to use intergovernmental agreements outside the EU legal order and stresses that these have set new rules on their entry into force which overcome state vetoes—suggesting that this is now a precedent to consider.

Chapter 6 considers the future of the EU beyond Brexit and analyses the plans, precedents, and prospects for the Conference on the Future of Europe. The establishment of the Conference on the Future of Europe is potentially an innovative model, and path-breaking initiative to reform the EU and make it more effective and legitimate—along the lines of prior, out-of-the-box initiatives such as the Conference of Messina and the Convention on the Future of Europe. The Covid-19 pandemic has delayed the start of the Conference on the Future of Europe, but it has also increased its urgency. However, the chances of success of this initiative are closely connected with the mechanics of treaty reform. As such, the chapter suggests that the Conference should consider channelling its output into a Political Compact, subject to entry into force rules that do away with the unanimity requirement, as has been done previously in the field of EMU. Clearly, success cannot be taken for granted, and there are many difficulties ahead—but the EU is facing a decisive moment.

Chapter 7, finally, concludes, emphasizing the connections between Brexit and EU reforms. The case for reforming the EU is not new. In recent years, multiple national and supranational leaders have put forward proposals to overhaul the EU and make it fit for the new challenges it faces.[12] Moreover, think tanks,[13] public intellectuals,[14] and academic scholars[15] have increasingly been reflecting on the future of Europe and suggesting plans ahead. This book joins this lively debate, but seeks to go beyond it by contributing ideas on how to move the EU forward, post-Covid-19. In particular, as the launch of the Conference on the Future of Europe approaches, this book not only supports this effort but also claims that this is an indispensable step following the UK's withdrawal from the EU. It also provides insights for policy-makers involved in the process, especially suggesting that a Political Compact for a more democratic and effective union can represent the avenue to relaunch the project of integration and renew Europe's future—*pace* Brexit.

[12] See e.g. Emmanuel Macron, *Revolution* (XO éditions 2016); and Guy Verhofstadt, *Europe's Last Chance: Why European States Must Form a More Perfect Union* (Basic Books 2017).

[13] See Björn Fägersten & Göran von Sydow (eds), 'Perspectives on the future of Europe', Swedish Institute for European Policy Studies report, April 2019; and Kirsty Hughes (ed), 'The Future of Europe: Disruption, Continuity and Change', Scottish Centre on European Relations report, May 2019.

[14] See Loukas Tsoukalis, *In Defence of Europe* (OUP 2016); and Ivan Krastev, *After Europe* (University of Pennsylvania Press 2017).

[15] See Sergio Fabbrini, *Europe's Future: Decoupling and Reforming* (CUP 2019); and Antonina Bakardjieva Engelbrekt & Xavier Groussot (eds), *The Future of Europe: Political and Legal Integration Beyond Brexit* (Hart Publishing 2019).

2

The EU during Brexit

The Withdrawal Negotiations

1. Introduction

The decision by the United Kingdom (UK) to leave the European Union (EU) started an unprecedented process for the EU institutions and the other Member States. While the EU heads of state and government in the European Council had been very generous in accommodating the pre-referendum requests of then UK Prime Minister David Cameron—by accepting, in February 2016, to give the UK a new, more special settlement in the EU[1]—the vote by the UK people to leave the EU in June 2016, and subsequently the notification by the UK government of its intention to withdraw from the EU in March 2017,[2] opened a new phase, as foreseen by Article 50 Treaty on European Union (TEU). The purpose of this chapter is to examine the EU during the Brexit negotiations, with the goal of shedding light on the reaction of the EU institutions and the other Member States, as well as on the implications that Brexit had on the EU policy agenda and its developments.

As the chapter argues, the EU institutions and the other Member States reacted to Brexit with remarkable unity—and this remained a distinctive feature of the EU stance during the entire withdrawal negotiations. On the one hand, the EU developed organizational arrangements which allowed it to negotiate with the UK as one; and on the other hand, the EU identified clear strategic priorities which were successfully taken forward in the Brexit process. However, Brexit also absorbed the energy of the

---

[1] See European Council Conclusions, 18–19 February 2016, EUCO 1/16, Annex I 'Decisions of the Heads of State or Government Meeting within the European Council concerning a New Settlement for the United Kingdom within the European Union'.
[2] Prime Minister Theresa May, Letter to European Council President Donald Tusk, 29 March 2017.

Brexit and the Future of the European Union. Federico Fabbrini, Oxford University Press (2020). © Federico Fabbrini. DOI: 10.1093/oso/9780198871262.003.0002

EU in other ways, as during the almost 44 months from the referendum to the eventual exit, the EU had to prepare for the opposite scenarios of a 'hard Brexit'—a case where the UK would leave with no deal—and of 'no Brexit'—a case where the UK would not leave, due to continuous requests to extend its EU membership ex Article 50(3) TEU. As the chapter explains, while ultimately neither of these scenarios materialized, Brexit featured prominently in the EU agenda during the withdrawal period, proving its salience for the EU.

At the same time, as the chapter underlines, Brexit served as a background for the launch of new constitutional debates and legislative developments within the EU. In particular, the remaining Member States started caucusing at 27, without the UK, to plan their future—leading to the rise of the 'EU27'. On the one hand, the EU27 kicked-off a debate on the future of Europe, designed to reflect on the prospects of integration in light of Brexit. On the other hand, they also exploited the decision of the UK to leave the EU to further advance integration in policy sectors, such as those of security and military affairs, where EU action had traditionally languished due to UK opposition. While during Brexit the debate on the future of Europe struggled to move from rhetoric to reality, and the operationalization of new policy initiatives was only partial, the opening of a reflection process and the development of new policy initiatives demonstrated the awareness among national and supranational leaders of the importance of responding to Brexit with a relaunch of the EU.

As such, this chapter is structured as follow. Section 2 focuses on the unity of the EU institutions and Member States during Brexit, analysing the organizational arrangements adopted by the EU to deal with the UK, and its strategic negotiating priorities—and showing how these allowed the EU successfully to achieve its objectives in the withdrawal process. Section 3 examines instead the EU between 'hard Brexit' and 'no Brexit'—discussing the work that the EU institutions and Member States had to put to prepare a no deal withdrawal, as well as to handle the subsequent UK requests to extend its EU membership. Section 4, instead, considers the emergence of the EU27 and explores how Brexit triggered both a debate on the future of Europe and the development of new policy initiative—and examines their significance even though in the course of the withdrawal process no concrete effort to reform the EU actually materialized. Section 5, finally, concludes.

2. The Unity of the EU

The EU responded to the result of the Brexit referendum of 23 June 2016 by embracing from the very beginning a united approach. The day after the referendum, the Presidents of the European Council, the European Parliament (EP), and the European Commission together with the Prime Minister of the Netherlands, which then held the rotating presidency of the Council, adopted a joint statement affirming that Brexit is 'an unprecedented situation but we are united in our response'.[3] The view was further developed on 29 June 2016, in an informal meeting of the 27 heads of state and government of the Member States (all except the UK), together with the Presidents of the European Council and the Commission: in a joint statement the leaders expressed their regret for the outcome of the referendum but confirmed their respect for the decision of the British people.[4] Moreover, they indicated their determination to 'remain united and work in the framework of the EU to deal with the challenges of the 21st century and find solutions in the interest of our nations and peoples'.[5] The unity of the EU in the Brexit negotiations reflected itself in the organizational arrangements adopted to manage the negotiations, as well as in the policy priorities set to guide talks with the UK.

2.1 Organizational Arrangements

From a very early stage, the EU started organizing to manage Brexit in an effective manner. In the 29 June 2016 statement, leaders emphasized the need to arrange an orderly withdrawal in accordance with the process enshrined in Article 50 TEU—and to this end they clarified that there would be no negotiation before the UK notification of its intention to leave the EU.[6] Moreover, the leaders indicated that as soon as the UK submitted its notification under Article 50 TEU, the European Council would adopt guidelines for the negotiations, and that the Commission and the EP

---

[3] Statement by the EU Leaders and the Netherlands Presidency of the outcome of the UK referendum, 24 June 2016.
[4] Informal meeting at 27, Statement, Brussels, 29 June 2016, para. 1.
[5] Ibid para. 5.
[6] Ibid para. 2.

would 'play their full role in accordance with the treaties'.[7] In fact, in July 2016 the Commission President Jean-Claude Juncker appointed Michel Barnier as Chief Negotiator of a newly constituted Task Force for the Preparation and Conduct of the Negotiations with the United Kingdom (so-called Task Force Article 50).[8] Furthermore, in September 2016, the EP appointed Guy Verhofstadt, a member of the EP Constitutional Affairs (AFCO) Committee and leader of the Alliance of Liberals and Democrats for Europe (ALDE), as leader of the EP Brexit steering group with responsibility for briefing the Conference of Presidents and developing the EP position on the matter.[9]

On 15 December 2016, in another informal meeting, the heads of state and government of the 27 together with the Presidents of the European Council and the Commission adopted procedural arrangements on how to manage the withdrawal negotiations.[10] Here, the leaders indicated that the European Council would 'set out the overall positions and principles that the EU will pursue throughout the negotiation' and remain 'permanently seized of the matter'.[11] However, the European Council confirmed that the Commission would be nominated as the EU negotiator vis-à-vis the UK,[12] and welcomed the appointment of Michel Barnier as Chief Negotiator.[13] Moreover, the European Council instructed the Council to swiftly adopt the decision authorizing the opening of the negotiations, and the detailed negotiating directives.[14] At the same time, the European Council invited the Commission as EU negotiator to keep 'the European Parliament closely and regularly informed throughout the negotiation',[15] reflecting the fact that under Article 50 TEU the EP had to consent to the withdrawal agreement.

---

[7] Ibid para. 3.
[8] See European Commission press release, 'President Juncker appoints Michel Barnier as Chief Negotiator', 27 July 2016, IP/16/2652.
[9] See European Parliament press release, 'Parliament appoints Guy Verhofstadt as representative on Brexit matters', 8 September 2016.
[10] Informal meeting of the Heads of State and Government of 27 Member States as well as the Presidents of the European Council and the European Commission, Brussels, 15 December 2016, Annex.
[11] Ibid para. 1.
[12] Ibid para. 3.
[13] Ibid.
[14] Ibid para. 2.
[15] Ibid para. 7.

As a result, when the UK eventually notified its intention to withdraw from the EU on 29 March 2017, the EU was fully ready.[16] Following the triggering of Article 50 TEU, on 31 March 2017 European Council President Donald Tusk published the draft guidelines for the negotiation with the UK, summarizing the proposed EU approach in handling, first, the divorce with the UK, and then the new relations with it.[17] On 5 April 2017, the EP gave its input on the strategy, identifying its red lines, and stressing that Article 50 TEU gave it the power to withhold its consent to any agreement with the UK, if this did not meet its requests.[18] Building on this, on 29 April 2017, the European Council, meeting at 27 without the UK, approved the political guidelines of the Brexit negotiations,[19] and on 3 May 2017 the Commission published its draft negotiating directives, detailing the European Council guidelines with a view towards starting negotiations with the UK.[20] These were then formally approved on 22 May 2017 by the Council, which authorized the Commission to start negotiations with the UK,[21] and simultaneously established a dedicated Council working party on Article 50 to follow the Commission's diplomatic work.[22]

The organizational arrangements adopted by the EU for the negotiations with the UK proved functional, and were preserved over time. In fact, the European Council was happy to set the strategic priorities, delegating all negotiations to the Commission—a trusted body with experience in handling international trade talks. At the same time, the Commission Task Force Article 50 led by Michel Barnier was able to build a solid relation of transparency and trust with the Council and the

---

[16] See also European Council, statement, 29 March 2017, 159/17.

[17] See General Secretariat of the Council, Draft guidelines following the United Kingdom's notification under Article 50 TEU, 31 March 2017, XT 21001/17.

[18] See European Parliament resolution of 5 April 2017 on negotiations with the United Kingdom following its notification that it intends to withdraw from the European Union, P8_TA(2017)0102.

[19] See European Council Guidelines, 29 April 2017, EUCO XT 20004/17.

[20] See European Commission, Recommendation for a Council Decision authorising the Commission to open negotiations on an agreement with the United Kingdom of Great Britain and Northern Ireland setting out the arrangements for its withdrawal from the European Union, 3 May 2017, COM(2017) 218 final.

[21] See Council Decision of 22 May 2017 authorising the opening of the negotiations with the United Kingdom of Great Britain and Northern Ireland for an agreement setting out the arrangements for its withdrawal from the European Union, Doc. XT 21016/17.

[22] See Council Decision of 22 May 2017 concerning the establishment of the ad hoc Working Party on Article 50 TEU chaired by the General Secretariat of the Council, Doc. XT 21017/17.

EP, both of which were kept closely informed and involved during the negotiations. As a result, the EU never divided vis-à-vis the UK during the almost three-year Brexit negotiations. Rather, both the Member States and the other EU institutions remained consistently united, delegating all talks with the UK to the ad hoc Commission Task Force Article 50, and backing the work of Chief Negotiator Barnier, who was explicitly thanked by the European Council on at least three occasions for his work of maintaining EU unity throughout the process.[23]

2.2 Strategic Priorities

The organizational arrangements adopted by the EU to deal with Brexit also allowed it to achieve its strategic objectives in the negotiations with the UK. Even before the start of the negotiations, top level EU officials began outlining the EU interests in the process, including preserving the integrity of the EU internal market.[24] Moreover, EU Member States most affected by Brexit quickly put forward their priorities: in particular, Ireland represented the challenges that a hard border with Northern Ireland would pose for the peace process in the island, and worked hard to make sure that its priorities would become those of the whole EU.[25] At the same time, the EU institutions aligned their positions, in the effort to best protect the interests of the EU against a withdrawing Member State. Pursuant to Article 50(2) TEU, it fell on the European Council to provide the guidelines for the negotiations and conclusion of the agreement with the withdrawing Member State. Nevertheless, the strategy of the European Council largely converged with that of the EP.

Hence, following the notification by the UK of its intention to withdraw from the EU, the EP adopted on 5 April 2017 a resolution where

---

[23] See European Council Conclusions, 25 November 2018, EUCO XT 20015/18, para. 3 (thanking 'Michel Barnier for his tireless efforts as the Union's chief negotiator and for maintaining the unity among EU27 Member States throughout the [Brexit] negotiations'); European Council Conclusions, 17 October 2019, EUCO XT 20018/19, para. 3; European Council Conclusions, 13 December 2019, EUCO XT 20027/19, para. 4.

[24] See e.g. Michel Barnier, Speech at the Committee of the Regions, 22 March 2017, as well as the European Commission non paper on key elements likely to feature in the draft negotiating directives, April 2017.

[25] See Government of Ireland, Brexit: Ireland's Priorities, 20 March 2017.

it set out its general principles on the negotiations,[26] which were largely echoed by the European Council in its 29 April 2017 guidelines.[27] In particular, the European Council affirmed that the EU's 'overall objective in these negotiations will be to preserve its interests, those of its citizens, its businesses and its Member States'.[28] Moreover, it stated that '[t]hroughout these negotiations the [EU] will maintain its unity and act as one with the aim of reaching a result that is fair and equitable for all Member States and in the interest of its citizens',[29] and categorically excluded 'separate negotiations between individual Member States and the United Kingdom on matters pertaining to the withdrawal'.[30] From a procedural point of view, the European Council set a phased approach, with negotiations on the withdrawal coming first, and negotiations on the framework of future EU–UK relations to be concluded only after the UK had subsequently become a third country, and only on the condition that 'sufficient progress has been made in the first phase'.[31]

From a substantive point of view, then, the European Council set out core principles for the first negotiating phase, stating that 'any agreement with the United Kingdom will have to be based on a balance of rights and obligations, and ensure a level playing field'.[32] Moreover, it clarified that a 'non-member of the [EU], that does not live up to the same obligations as a member, cannot have the same rights and enjoy the same benefits as a member', and excluded any possibility of cherry-picking.[33] Finally, it also identified policy priorities for the negotiations, including protecting the rights of EU citizens in the UK, and UK citizens in the EU; settling the financial obligations owed by the UK at the time of exit; and avoiding a hard border between Ireland and Northern Ireland in 'view of the unique circumstances of the island of Ireland'.[34]

---

[26] European Parliament resolution of 5 April 2017 on negotiations with the United Kingdom following its notification that it intends to withdraw from the European Union (n 18).
[27] European Council Guidelines (n 19).
[28] Ibid.
[29] Ibid.
[30] Ibid para. 2.
[31] Ibid para. 5.
[32] Ibid para. 1.
[33] Ibid para. 2.
[34] Ibid para. 11.

As the negotiations then moved on to the second phase—following the December 2017 UK–EU Joint report,[35] and the acknowledgement that sufficient progress had been made on the first phase[36]—the European Council added new guidelines on the UK proposal for a transition period,[37] as well as on the contours of the future EU–UK relations.[38] Once again, the EP also advanced its articulated position on the matter in a resolution of 14 March 2018, where it proposed an association agreement as the framework for the EU's relations with the UK post-Brexit.[39] And on 23 March 2018, the European Council adopted additional, more detailed guidelines on the negotiations on the framework of future EU–UK relations, where it stated its 'determination to have as close as possible a partnership with the UK in the future',[40] spanning from trade to security cooperation. From a substantive point of view, moreover, the European Council reaffirmed that as a third country the UK could not aspire to the same levels of benefits of a Member State, and reaffirmed the indivisibility of the four freedoms, the importance of preserving the EU decision-making autonomy, as well as to respect the role of the European Court of Justice (ECJ) in the framework of the future relations.[41]

In sum, throughout the negotiation process, the EU was able to impose its policy priorities and successfully leverage its strength by remaining united vis-à-vis the UK. Otherwise, as has been pointed out, the final Withdrawal Agreement[42] largely tracked the preferences of the EU—notwithstanding the changes that were negotiated by the Johnson government after the deal originally struck by the May government was rejected three times by the UK Parliament.[43] If this outcome also reflected the much greater political and economic weight of the EU compared to that

---

[35] See Joint report from the negotiators of the European Union and the United Kingdom Government on progress during phase 1 of negotiations under Article 50 TEU on the United Kingdom's orderly withdrawal from the European Union, 8 December 2017, TF50(2017)19.

[36] See European Council Guidelines, 15 December 2017, EUCO XT 20011/17, para. 1.

[37] Ibid para. 3.

[38] Ibid para. 6.

[39] European Parliament resolution of 14 March 2018 on the framework of the future EU-UK relationship, P8_TA(2018)69.

[40] European Council Guidelines, 23 March 2018, EUCO XT 20001/18, para. 3.

[41] Ibid para. 7.

[42] Agreement on the withdrawal of the United Kingdom of Great Britain and Northern Ireland from the European Union and the European Atomic Energy Community, OJ 2020 L 29/07.

[43] See Emily Jones, 'The Negotiations' in Federico Fabbrini (ed), *The Law & Politics of Brexit: Volume II: The Withdrawal Agreement* (OUP 2020), 37.

of the UK—a recurrent driver in explaining the results of international trade negotiations—the way how the EU handled the Brexit process were also a testament of the ability of the EU institutions and its Member States to stick together in the face of a country which had decided to leave the EU, with the aim of preserving the achievements of integration against possible free-riding behaviours, as well as to protect the interest of its weaker members.[44]

3. Between 'Hard Brexit' and 'No Brexit'

Brexit had a number of implications for the EU, as it sought to prepare itself for a new reality without the UK.[45] In particular, during the withdrawal process, besides negotiating with the UK, the EU faced a twin risk. On the one hand, the EU had to prepare for a so-called 'hard Brexit' scenario—a case of no deal where the UK would leave the EU at the end of the two-year period after the notification of Article 50 TEU without a withdrawal agreement. On the other hand, the EU also had to face a 'no Brexit' scenario[46]—as a result of subsequent requests by the UK to postpone the exit day and extend its membership of the EU ex Article 50(3) TEU. In the end, neither of these scenarios materialized as the UK left the EU on 31 January 2020 on the basis of an orderly withdrawal agreement, which received the consent of the EP[47] and was concluded by the Council on behalf of the EU.[48] However, during the three-year Brexit

---

[44] See Irish Taoiseach Leo Varadkar, 'Thank you to the People of Europe', Op-Ed, *Irish Times*, 31 January 2020 (expressing gratitude to the EU and its Member States for standing in solidarity with Ireland throughout the Brexit process).

[45] Because of the outcome of the Brexit referendum, instead, the 'New Settlement for the UK within the EU', agreed by the European Council in February 2016, was scrapped. See European Council Conclusions (n 1) para. 4 (stating that the arrangements agreed with the UK will cease to exist 'should the result of the referendum in the United Kingdom be for it to leave the EU').

[46] Indeed, on 10 December 2018 the ECJ removed any doubt that under EU law the UK had the right to withdraw its notification under Article 50 TEU of its intention to leave the EU. See Case C-621/18 *Wightman*, ECLI:EU:C:2018:999.

[47] See European Parliament legislative resolution of 29 January 2020 on the draft Council decision on the conclusion of the Agreement on the Withdrawal of the United Kingdom of Great Britain and Northern Ireland from the European Union and the European Atomic Energy Community, P9_TA(2020)0018.

[48] See Council Decision (EU) 2020/135 of 30 January 2020 on the conclusion of the withdrawal of the United Kingdom of Great Britain and Northern Ireland from the European Union and the European Economic Energy Community, OJ 2020 L 29/1.

negotiations, the EU institutions and the Member States had repeatedly to dedicate their energies and attention to the matter.

3.1   Preparations

Immediately after the Brexit referendum, the EU institutions had to deal with the fall-out of the vote. The Council changed the order of the rotating presidencies,[49] in order to reflect the decision by the UK to waive its turn for the second half of 2017. Moreover, following the resignation of the UK-nominated Commissioner, the Council duly appointed another Commissioner in respect of the UK, to whom the Commission assigned a new portfolio in a reshuffling of cabinet responsibilities.[50] At the same time, the Commission started putting forward proposals for amendments to EU legislation designed to adjust the *acquis communautaire* to the withdrawal of the UK from the EU. For example, the EU adopted legislation to amend the Connecting Europe Facility and include Ireland (rather than the UK) in the Ten-T networks;[51] it updated in the field of financial services the procedures and authorities involved for the authorization of central counterparties (CCPs) and requirements for the recognition of third-country CCPs;[52] and it revised the rules on the composition of the EP—which will be analysed in depth in Chapter 3.

[49] See Council Decision (EU) 2016/1316 of 26 July 2016 amending Decision 2009/908/EU, laying down measures for the implementation of the European Council Decision on the exercise of the Presidency of the Council, and on the chairmanship of preparatory bodies of the Council, OJ 2016 L 208/42.

[50] See European Commission statement on the Decision of Commissioner Lord Hill to resign from the Commission and on the transfer of the Financial Service portfolio to Vice-President Dombrovskis, 25 June 2016, 16/2332 and Council of the EU press release, 'Julian King appointed new commissioner for security union', 19 September 2016.

[51] See Regulation (EU) 2019/495 of the European Parliament and of the Council of 25 March 2019 amending Regulation (EU) No 1316/2013 with regard to the withdrawal of the United Kingdom from the Union, OJ 2019 L 851/16.

[52] Regulation (EU) 2019/2099 of the European Parliament and of the Council of 23 October 2019 amending Regulation (EU) No 648/2012 as regards the procedures and authorities involved for the authorisation of CCPs and requirements for the recognition of third-country CCPs, OJ 2019 L 322/1. In 2015, the UK had successfully challenged a European Central Bank (ECB) decision 'in so far as it sets a requirement to be located within a Member State party to the Eurosystem for central counterparties involved in the clearing of securities'. See Case T-496/11 *UK v ECB*, ECLI:EU:T:2015:133. Following Brexit, the Commission put forward a proposal that would have reintroduced the location requirement. See European Commission Proposal for a Regulation of the European Parliament and the Council amending Regulation (EU) No 1095/2010 establishing a European Supervisory Authority (European Securities and Markets Authority) and amending Regulation (EU) No 648/2012 as regards the procedures and

In addition, the EU institutions and Member States also tackled the issue of the relocation of EU agencies based in the UK—the European Banking Authority (EBA) and the European Medical Agency (EMA)—which turned out to be the most contentious issue for the EU, and certainly the only one on which the Member States lost their unity. On 22 June 2017, on the margin of the European Council, leaders agreed on a procedure leading up to a decision on the relocation of the EBA and the EMA.[53] The procedure was designed to guarantee the agencies' business continuity, and was based on a bidding process by Member States, to be first evaluated by the Commission in light of several criteria and then voted on by the Council though a complex subsequent round of voting and with the ultimate option of deciding by lot to break a tie. In the end, following this procedure, in November 2017 the Council supported the relocation of the EBA to Paris[54] and of the EMA to Amsterdam.[55] Nevertheless, the latter vote, and its implementation,[56] was challenged before the ECJ on the grounds of false information by the runner-up in the adjudication—Milan, which had tied with the winner and only lost by lot.[57]

Nevertheless, the EU also invested significant resources into preparing for a 'hard Brexit' scenario, with the UK exiting the EU two years after the notification of its intention to leave without a deal. Given the difficulties in the negotiations with the UK, the Commission advanced preparations for a 'hard Brexit', releasing a series of contingency planning

authorities involved for the authorisation of CCPs and requirements for the recognition of third-country CCPs, 13 June 2017, COM(2017) 0331 final. In the end, Art. 25 of Regulation (EU) 2019/2099 empowered the European Securities and Markets Authority (ESMA) to assess the 'degree of systemic importance of the CCP [... and], on the basis of a fully reasoned assessment, conclude that a CCP or some of its clearing services are of such substantial systemic importance that that CCP should not be recognised to provide certain clearing services or activities'.

[53] See Procedure leading up to a decision on the relocation of the European Medicines Agency and the European Banking Authority in the context of the United Kingdom's withdrawal from the Union, 22 June 2017.

[54] Council of the EU press release, 'European Banking Authority to be relocated to Paris, France', 20 November 2017, 689/17.

[55] Council of the EU press release, 'European Medicine Agency to be relocated to Amsterdam, the Netherlands', 20 November 2017, 688/17.

[56] See Regulation (EU) 2018/1718 of the European Parliament and of the Council of 14 November 2018 amending Regulation (EC) No 726/2004 as regards the location of the seat of the European Medicines Agency, OJ 2018 L 291/3.

[57] See Case C-106/19 *Italy v Council and Parliament*, pending.

documents—starting in summer 2018,[58] intensifying in autumn 2018,[59] and continuing during 2019[60]—which invited citizens and businesses to get ready for Brexit.[61] Moreover, the Commission adopted a temporary and conditional equivalence decision in the field of financial services for a fixed, limited period of time to ensure that there would be no immediate disruption in the central clearing of derivatives,[62] and also put forward contingency legislation, which was approved by the EP and the Council, to ensure the continuity of some operations in the case of a no deal Brexit, including basic road freight connectivity[63] and social security coordination.[64] In fact, while the EU started preparing also for the consequences that Brexit would have on the EU budget—which will be analysed in Chapter 3—it also adopted contingency legislation to mobilize the European Globalisation Adjustment Fund to support people who may lose their jobs as a result of a no deal Brexit.[65]

At the same time, reflections also took place within the EU on the consequences of a 'hard Brexit' for the EU institutions and their members. On

---

[58] European Commission Communication, 'Preparing for the withdrawal of the United Kingdom from the European Union on 30 March 2019', 19 July 2018, COM(2018) 556 final.

[59] European Commission Communication, 'Preparing for the withdrawal of the United Kingdom from the European Union on 30 March 2019: A Contingency Action Plan', 13 November 2018, COM(2018) 880 final; and European Commission Communication, 'Preparing for the withdrawal of the United Kingdom from the European Union on 30 March 2019: Implementing the Commission's Contingency Action Plan', 19 December 2018, COM(2018) 890 final.

[60] European Commission Communication, 'Addressing the Impact of a Withdrawal of the United Kingdom from the Union without an agreement: the Union's coordinated approach', 19 April 2019, COM(2019) 195 final; European Commission Communication, 'State of play of preparations of contingency measures for the withdrawal of the United Kingdom from the European Union', 12 June 2019, COM(2019) 276 final.

[61] See also the campaign of the Government of Ireland, 'Getting Ireland Brexit ready' https://www.dfa.ie/brexit/about/.

[62] See Commission Implementing Decision (EU) 2018/2031 of 19 December 2018 determining, for a limited period of time, that the regulatory framework applicable to central counterparties in the United Kingdom of Great Britain and Northern Ireland is equivalent, in accordance with Regulation (EU) No 648/2012 of the European Parliament and of the Council, OJ 2018 L 325, subsequently amended twice.

[63] See Regulation (EU) 2019/501 of the European Parliament and of the Council of 25 March 2019 on common rules ensuring basic road freight and road passenger connectivity with regard to the withdrawal of the United Kingdom of Great Britain and Northern Ireland from the Union, OJ 2019 L 85I/39.

[64] See Regulation (EU) 2019/500 of the European Parliament and of the Council of 25 March 2019 establishing contingency measures in the field of social security coordination following the withdrawal of the United Kingdom from the Union, OJ 2019 L 85I/35.

[65] See Regulation (EU) 2019/1796 of the European Parliament and of the Council of 24 October 2019 amending Regulation (EU) No 1309/2013 on the European Globalisation Adjustment Fund (2014-2020), OJ 2019 L 279I/4.

the one hand, a discussion occurred on the fate of EU officials holding UK nationality.[66] On the other hand, questions arose about the consequences for the EU institutions as such. In particular, in a report commissioned by the EP AFCO Committee, I explored the implications of a no-deal Brexit, and suggested that, even though the UK representation in the Council, the European Council, and the Commission would automatically terminate on exit day, on the contrary, UK-elected members of the EP and UK-appointed judges and advocate general at the ECJ were entitled to maintain their functions until the natural end of their mandates, given that their constitutional function was not one of state representation.[67] Yet, while the matter was contested,[68] in the end, the hypothesis of a 'hard Brexit' did not materialize, as the UK eventually left the EU on the basis of a mutually agreed withdrawal agreement—but only after extending its membership in the EU a little longer.

3.2   Extensions

While the UK was due to leave the EU on 29 March 2019, given the failure to secure ratification of the withdrawal deal in the UK Parliament, the UK government eventually triggered in March 2019 the facility foreseen in Article 50(3) TEU, seeking an extension of UK membership in the EU. Moreover, the UK government subsequently requested further extensions twice more during 2019, which ultimately led the UK to leave the EU almost 10 months later than originally planned. This forced the European Council to decide on the UK's requests, and by doing so also to develop a practice on Article 50(3) TEU. In fact, as Rebecca Schmidt and I have explained elsewhere,[69] Article 50(3) TEU only regulates extension in procedural terms, by requiring that an extension is decided

---

[66] See also Herwig Hofmann, 'The impact of Brexit on the legal status of European Union officials and other servants of British nationality', study commissioned by the European Parliament Constitutional Affairs Committee, December 2017.

[67] See Federico Fabbrini, 'The Institutional Consequences of a "Hard Brexit"', study commissioned by the European Parliament Constitutional Affairs Committee, May 2018.

[68] See Miguel Tell Cremades & Petr Novak, 'Brexit and the European Union: General Institutional and Legal Considerations', study commissioned by the European Parliament Constitutional Affairs Committee, January 2017.

[69] See Federico Fabbrini & Rebecca Schmidt, 'The Extensions' in Federico Fabbrini (ed), *The Law & Politics of Brexit: Volume II: The Withdrawal Agreement* (OUP 2020), 66.

by the European Council (i) unanimously, and (ii) in agreement with the withdrawing Member State. Nevertheless, the European Council is under no legal obligation to grant an extension, and as such it is empowered to introduce conditions when taking such a decision—provided these are not incompatible with EU primary law—which is what the European Council did on all three extension requests it received from the UK.

The European Council decided on the first extension request from the UK government—formalized on 20 March 2019, and seeking to postpone the exit date to 30 June 2019, with the aim of buying time to make another attempt at ratifying the withdrawal deal in the UK Parliament[70]—by adopting a decision on 22 March 2019. Here, after balancing the options of a short, technical extension as opposed to a longer, political one, the European Council accepted the UK's request. However, aware of the legal and political difficulties that an extension would create on the approaching EP elections,[71] the European Council only granted an extension until 12 April 2019 (the last date by which the UK had to organize the holding of EP elections), unless the UK Parliament approved the withdrawal agreement before that date.[72] Yet, the UK Parliament rejected the draft deal a third time on 29 March 2019—the day when the UK was originally expected to leave the EU—and, as a result, the UK government on 5 April 2019 sent a letter to the European Council President asking a second time for an extension, once again until 30 June 2019.[73]

The European Council decided on the second extension request from the UK government by adopting a decision on 11 April 2019.[74] Here, the European Council accepted the UK's request, but rejected the UK's timeframe and instead set a flexible deadline.[75] Specifically, the European Council stated that '[s]uch an extension should last as long as necessary

---

[70] See Prime Minister Theresa May, Letter to European Council President Donald Tusk, 20 March 2019.

[71] See European Commission President Jean-Claude Juncker, Letter to European Council President Donald Tusk, 11 March 2019 (stating that the UK exit 'should be complete before the European Parliament elections that will take place between 23-26 May [2019]. If the United Kingdom has not left the European Union by then, it will be legally required to hold these elections, in line with the rights and obligations of all Member States as set out in the Treaties'.)

[72] European Council Decision (EU) 2019/476 taken in agreement with the United Kingdom of 22 March 2019 extending the period under Article 50(3) TEU, OJ 2019 L 80 I/1.

[73] See Prime Minister May, Letter to European Council President Donald Tusk, 5 April 2019.

[74] See European Council Decision (EU) 2019/584 taken in agreement with the United Kingdom of 11 April 2019 extending the period under Article 50(3) TEU, OJ 2019 L 101/1.

[75] Ibid recital 9.

and, in any event, no longer than 31 October 2019'.[76] Moreover, the European Council clarified that the extension would end, with an automatic UK withdrawal on 1 June 2019, if the UK was still a member of the EU on 23–26 May 2019, and had failed to hold elections to the EP.[77] At the same time, the European Council stressed the UK's responsibility as a continuous Member State of the EU, clarifying that '[t]his further extension cannot be allowed to undermine the regular functioning of the Union and its institutions'.[78] In this regard, the European Council took note of the 'commitment by the United Kingdom to act in a constructive and responsible manner throughout the extension period in accordance with the duty of sincere cooperation'[79] and stressed that it

> expects the United Kingdom to fulfil this commitment and Treaty obligation in a manner that reflects its situation as a withdrawing Member State. To this effect, the United Kingdom shall facilitate the achievement of the Union's tasks and shall refrain from any measure which could jeopardise the attainment of the Union's objectives, in particular when participating in the decision-making processes of the Union.[80]

Finally, the European Council decided on a third extension request from the UK government on 29 October 2019. This request—which resulted from the application of the Benn Act[81] imposing an obligation on the UK Prime Minister to seek an extension until 31 January 2020 if a deal had not been approved by the UK Parliament by 19 October 2019[82]— was approved through a written procedure by a simple meeting of the Permanent Representatives of the 27 Member States, without calling a special in-person meeting of the European Council.[83] In its decision, the European Council approved the UK request for extension of membership

---

[76] Ibid.
[77] Ibid recital 10.
[78] Ibid.
[79] Ibid.
[80] Ibid.
[81] European Union (Withdrawal) Act (No 2) 2019 (UK).
[82] See Letter from the UK to the EU Council, 19 October 2019. See also UK Permanent Representative to the EU Sir Tim Barrow, Letter to Secretary General of the Council of the EU Jeppe Tranholm-Mikkelsen, 19 October 2019.
[83] European Council Decision (EU) 2019/1810 taken in agreement with the United Kingdom of 28 October 2019 extending the period under Article 50(3) TEU, OJ 2019 L 278I.

until 31 January 2020. Just like the previous one, the third extension also included a flexibility clause, according to which the UK could leave the EU before 31 January 2020 if it ratified the withdrawal agreement beforehand.[84] The decision explicitly stated that the extension was adopted 'with a view to allowing for the finalization of the ratification of the withdrawal agreement'.[85] This was also restated in a separate declaration by the EU heads of state and government,[86] which also excluded 'any re-opening of the Withdrawal Agreement in the future'.[87] Moreover, like the prior decisions, the third one also pointed out that the UK 'will remain a Member State until the new withdrawal date, with full rights and obligations'.[88] It thus also required the UK 'to suggest a candidate for appointment as member of the Commission',[89] and more generally recalled 'the commitment by the [UK] to act in a constructive and responsible manner throughout the extension period in accordance with the duty of sincere cooperation'.[90]

In conclusion, by adopting its extension decisions the European Council exercised its prerogatives as the institution in charge of steering the withdrawal process, averting a 'hard Brexit' while also advancing conditions to regulate the postponement of exit. And yet, there is no denying that the Brexit extension represented a distraction for the EU. UK Prime Minister Boris Johnson himself recognized as much, when he regretted with European Council President Tusk—in a personal letter sent to the sides of the third extension request (de facto forced on him by the Benn Act)—that heads of state and governments had to devote more time and energy to Brexit and expressed his views that a new delay in the withdrawal of the UK 'would damage the interests of the UK and the EU partners'.[91] Moreover, the extensions of UK membership in the EU were not without institutional consequences for the EU, as they created

---

[84] Ibid Art. 1(2).
[85] Ibid recital 9.
[86] See Declaration of the European Council, 29 October 2019, EUCO XT 20025/1/19.
[87] Ibid.
[88] European Council Decision 2019/1810 (n 83) recital 11.
[89] Ibid.
[90] Ibid.
[91] Prime Minister Boris Johnson, Letter to European Council President Donald Tusk, 19 October 2019.

transitional issues and novel challenges—which will be analysed in depth in Chapter 3.

4. The Emergence of the EU27

The Brexit referendum quickly pushed all the other 27 EU Member States to meet together without the UK—leading to the emergence of the so-called 'EU27'. In fact, the grouping of the remaining Member States soon moved beyond informality: not only under Article 50(4) TEU was the UK excluded from participating in European Council and Council meetings concerning the withdrawal process, but de facto the EU27 also sought to discuss by themselves matters which concerned the future of the EU. Indeed, when adopting the second extension decision in April 2019, the European Council also pointed out that, where appropriate, the other 27 EU Member States 'will continue to meet separately at all levels to discuss matters related to the [EU] situation after the withdrawal of the United Kingdom'.[92] It is within this framework at 27, that the EU institutions and Member States also started debating the future of Europe, and developed new policy initiatives.

4.1 The Debate on the Future of Europe

The conversation on the future of Europe started immediately after the Brexit referendum. In a resolution adopted on 28 June 2016, just five days after the Brexit referendum, the EP took notice of the decision of the UK to leave the EU and stressed that 'the current challenges require reflection on the future of the EU: there is a need to reform the Union and make it better and more democratic'.[93] In particular, the EP noted that 'while some Member States may choose to integrate more slowly or to a lesser extent, the core of the EU must be reinforced and à la carte solutions should be avoided'[94]—and it simultaneously identified a host of

---

[92] See European Council Conclusions, 10 April 2019, EUCO XT 20015/19, para. 8.
[93] European Parliament resolution of 28 June 2016 on the decision to leave the EU resulting from the UK referendum, P8_TA(2016)0294, para. 10.
[94] Ibid.

policy areas where 'reforms must result in a Union which delivers what citizens expect'.[95] To this end, the EP called for 'a roadmap for a better Union based on exploiting the Lisbon Treaty to the full, to be completed by a revision of the Treaties'.[96] Moreover, on 29 June 2016, the leaders of the EU27 affirmed that they would start 'a political reflection to give an impulse to further reforms ... and to the development of the EU with 27 Member States'.[97] In a declaration concluded in Bratislava, Slovakia, on 16 September 2016, the EU27 endorsed a roadmap designed to reflect on the future of Europe, and identify priorities for action.[98]

In fact, while proposals to reform the EU had proliferated during the euro-crisis,[99] a further boost for the debate on EU constitutional reform occurred on the occasion of the celebrations of the 60th anniversary of the Treaties of Rome in March 2017. As this historic moment arrived exactly at the time when the UK triggered Article 50 TEU, the EU institutions and the Member States sought to reflect on how to absorb the loss of the UK while charting a new way forward. In particular, on 1 March 2017, the Commission published a white paper on the future of the EU.[100] The white paper, which was then integrated by several sector-specific reflection papers,[101] outlined five alternative scenarios for the EU's future: (1) carrying on; (2) nothing but the single market; (3) those who want more do more; (4) doing less more efficiently; and (5) doing much more together. These scenarios were presented to the Member States for consideration, but the Commission did not itself outline its preferences for the way forward—although Commission President Jean-Claude Juncker articulated his view for a stronger, more united, and more democratic union in his state of the union addresses before the EP in 2017,[102] which

[95] Ibid.

[96] Ibid para. 11.

[97] Informal meeting at 27 (n 4) para. 7.

[98] See Bratislava Declaration, 16 September 2016.

[99] See e.g. Four Presidents' report, 'Towards a Genuine EMU', 5 December 2012; and Five Presidents' report, 'Completing Europe's EMU', 22 June 2015.

[100] European Commission white paper, 'The Future of Europe', 1 March 2017.

[101] See e.g. European Commission reflection paper on 'The social dimension of Europe', 26 April 2017; European Commission reflection paper on 'Harnessing globalization', 10 May 2017; and European Commission reflection paper on 'The Deepening of Economic and Monetary Union', 31 May 2017.

[102] European Commission President Jean-Claude Juncker, State of the Union Address 2017, Brussels, 13 September 2017.

was echoed in 2018 by a call for European sovereignty as a vision for the future.[103]

Instead, a very consistent view for constitutional reform in the EU after Brexit has been expressed by the EP. In particular, in February 2017 the EP approved a set of resolutions which combined calls for a greater exploitation of the legal and institutional mechanisms currently available under the Treaties, while also outlining a roadmap for treaty reforms ahead. On the one hand, the EP claimed that the action should be taken *à traité constant*, with further integration in the area of economic governance, social policy, and defence.[104] Moreover, the EP reaffirmed its intention to set up a fiscal capacity for the EU, based on real EU taxes,[105] as indicated also in the final report of the High-level Group on Own Resources chaired by former Italian Prime Minister and European Commissioner Mario Monti.[106] On the other hand, however, the EP also unveiled its plans for constitutional changes beyond the Treaty of Lisbon, aimed at overhauling more fundamentally the EU institutional architecture,[107] and it emphasized how Brexit should be used to this end.[108]

Heads of state and government, finally, also debated the future of the EU and, on 25 March 2017, they signed together with the Presidents of the European Council, the Commission and the EP a declaration in Rome pledging their support for European integration and defining the 'Union [a]s undivided and indivisible'.[109] While this declaration was mostly focused on celebrating the achievements of 60 years of European integration, it indicated space for future cooperation in the field of internal security, economic growth, and social protection, as well as foreign policy and defence. The declaration avoided any discussion of the

---

[103] European Commission President Jean-Claude Juncker, State of the Union Address 2018, Brussels, 12 September 2018.

[104] See European Parliament resolution of 16 February 2017 on improving the functioning of the European Union building on the potential of the Lisbon Treaty, P8_TA(2017)0049.

[105] See European Parliament resolution of 16 February 2017 on budgetary capacity for the Eurozone, P8_TA(2017)0050.

[106] See Mario Monti, High-level Group on Own Resources, final report and recommendations, 'Future Financing of the EU', December 2016.

[107] See European Parliament resolution of 16 February 2017 on possible evolutions of and adjustments to the current institutional set-up of the European Union, P8_TA(2017)0048.

[108] See also European Parliament resolution of 5 April 2017 on negotiations with the United Kingdom following its notification that it intends to withdraw from the European Union (n 18).

[109] Rome Declaration of the leaders of 27 Member States and of the European Council, the European Parliament and the European Commission, 25 March 2017.

legal and institutional mechanisms to achieve these objectives, and con-
tented itself with proclaiming that the EU Member States and institutions
will 'promote a democratic, effective and transparent decision-making
process and better delivery'. Nevertheless, the compromise did not obfuscate the calls—notably by the Italian President,[110] and the speakers of
parliaments of 14 EU Member States[111] for immediate treaty changes to
establish a federal union endowed with adequate powers and democratic
legitimacy.

In fact, the debate on the future of Europe continued thereafter
under the strategic guidance of the European Council—as the institution responsible ex Article 15 TEU for defining the general political direction of the EU—with the effort to chart a united way forward at 27.
In October 2017, in particular, European Council President Donald
Tusk launched a new working method known as the 'Leaders Agenda',
which foresaw a more structured conversation among leaders around
thematic issues—including migration, trade, internal and external security, and economic affairs—with the aim of 'resolving deadlocks or
finding solutions to key political dossiers'.[112] In November 2017, the
EU27 gathered in Goteborg, Sweden, to proclaim the European Pillar
of Social Rights, a set of 20 non-binding principles designed to re-
affirm the EU commitment to a social Europe. Moreover, under the
leadership of EP President Antonio Tajani, in the build-up to the EP
elections, 16 heads of state and government of the EU27—starting with
Irish Taoiseach Leo Varadkar in January 2018[113]—were invited to present their vision of the future of Europe in front of the EP,[114] which

---

[110] See Italian President Sergio Mattarella, 'I valori dell'Europa', intervento in occasione della
seduta congiunta delle Camere per il 60° anniversario dei Trattati di Roma, Rome, 22 March
2017 (speaking of the need to relaunch 'la riforma dei Trattati').

[111] See President of the French Assemblé Nationale Claude Bertolone, President of the Italian
Camera dei Deputati Laura Boldrini, President of the German Bundestag Norbert Lammert
et al, 'Un patto per l'Unione federale', La Stampa, 26 February 2012.

[112] European Council, Leaders Agenda, 17 October 2017.

[113] Irish Taoiseach Leo Varadkar, speech Strasbourg, 17 January 2018.

[114] Croatian PM Andrej Plankovic, speech Strasbourg, 6 February 2018; Portuguese PM
Antonio Costa, speech Strasbourg, 14 March 2018; French President Emmanuel Macron,
speech Strasbourg, 17 April 2018; Belgian PM Charles Michel, speech Strasbourg, 3 May 2018;
Luxembourg PM Xavier Bettel, speech Strasbourg, 30 May 2018; Dutch PM Mark Rutte, speech
Strasbourg, 13 June 2018; Polish PM Mateusz Morawiecki, speech Strasbourg, 4 July 2018;
Greek PM Alexis Tsipras, speech Strasbourg, 11 September 2018; Estonian PM Juri Ratas,
speech Strasbourg, 3 October 2018; Romanian President Klaus Iohannis, speech Strasbourg,

also then adopted its position on the state of the debate on the future of Europe.[115]

This process of reflection culminated in a special summit held on Europe Day, 9 May 2019, in Sibiu, Romania, where EU leaders approved a declaration on the future of Europe.[116] Days before the 9th EP elections, the Presidents of the EU political institutions and the heads of state and government of the EU27 reaffirmed their conviction that 'united, we are stronger in this increasingly unsettled and challenging world'[117] and spelled out 10 commitments 'of a new Union at 27 ready to embrace its future as one'.[118] The first among these commitments was a pledge, echoing the Declaration on the Reunification of Europe signed in Warsaw on 1 May 2019 by the 13 new Member States that had joined the EU since 2004,[119] to 'defend one Europe—from East to West, from North to South',[120] honouring the 30th anniversary of the fall of the Iron Curtain and the 15th anniversary of the major enlargement into Central and Eastern Europe. Furthermore, on the same day, the heads of state of 21 Member States (those with an elected president rather than a monarch) signed a joint call for Europe ahead of the EP elections, which stated that 'unity is essential and that we want to continue Europe as a Union'.[121]

Nevertheless, the debate on the future of Europe struggled to move from rhetoric to reality during the time of the Brexit negotiations. While the framework of the debate on the future of Europe allowed the Commission to engage in a broad exercise of citizens' dialogues and consultations,[122] the process did not materialize into any concrete reform.

23 October 2018; German Chancellor Angela Merkel, speech Strasbourg, 13 November 2018; Danish PM Lars Lokke Rasmussen, speech Strasbourg, 28 November 2018; Cypriot President Nicos Anastasiades, speech Strasbourg, 12 December 2018; Spanish PM Pedro Sanchez, speech Strasbourg, 16 January 2019; Finnish PM Juha Sipilä, speech Strasbourg, 31 January 2019; Italian President of the Council Giuseppe Conte, speech Strasbourg, 12 February 2019, Slovak PM Peter Pellegrini, speech Strasbourg, 7 March 2019; Swedish PM Stefan Lofven, speech Strasbourg, 3 April 2019; Latvian PM Krišjānis Kariņš, speech Strasbourg, 17 April 2019.

[115] See European Parliament resolution of 13 February 2019 on the state of the debate on the future of Europe, P8_TA(2019)0098.
[116] Sibiu Declaration, 9 May 2019.
[117] Ibid.
[118] Ibid.
[119] See Warsaw Declaration on the Reunification of Europe, 1 May 2019.
[120] Sibiu Declaration, 9 May 2019.
[121] Joint Call for Europe ahead of the European Parliament elections in May 2019, 9 May 2019.
[122] European Commission, 'Citizens' Dialogues and Citizens' Consultations: Key Conclusions', 30 April 2019.

Otherwise, the debate on the future of Europe also failed to create sufficient consensus among the EU27 on the EU policy priorities going forward, as evidenced by the European Council adoption in June 2019 of a new strategic agenda.[123] This roadmap, which followed the EP elections that will be analysed in Chapter 3 and was meant to bring the debate on Europe's future to a climax,[124] however lacked detail as a condition to keep all Member States on board—and therefore revealed the profound difference between the EU27 Member States' visions on the future of Europe. This latter aspect will be analysed in Chapter 4.

In fact, repeated calls to unity from the Bratislava Declaration, to the Rome Declaration and the Sibiu Declaration, were met with countervailing pressures. On the one hand, this period of time saw the consolidations of powerful regional blocs, which often put forward conflicting visions of the EU's future. The prospect of the UK's withdrawal from the EU also prompted an increasing effort by Member States to regroup and rebuild alliances for a post-Brexit EU. On the other hand, the most ambitious proposals for the relaunch of the EU arguably came from national, as opposed to EU, leaders. In particular, French President Emmanuel Macron advanced an ambitious vision for the future of Europe. In his speech at Sorbonne University in September 2017, he made a passionate case in favour of a real European sovereignty as a way for the EU to face the challenges of the new century[125]—a point he subsequently repeated also in May 2018, when receiving the Prix Charlemagne,[126] and in November 2018, when speaking in the Bundestag on the occasion of the 100th anniversary of the end of the First World War.[127] Indeed, his energy and foresight were instrumental in March 2019 in advancing a proposal

---

[123] See European Council Conclusions, 20 June 2019, EUCO 9/19, Annex I: A New Strategic Agenda.

[124] See also European Commission contribution to the informal EU27 leaders' meeting in Sibiu Romania on 9 May 2019, 'Europe in May 2019: Preparing for a more united stronger and more democratic Union in an increasingly uncertain world', 30 April 2019.

[125] French President Emmanuel Macron, speech at Université La Sorbonne, Paris, 26 September 2017.

[126] French President Emmanuel Macron, speech at the award of the Prix Charlemagne, Aachen, 11 May 2018.

[127] French President Emmanuel Macron, speech at the Bundestag on the commemoration of the 100th anniversary of the end of the First World War, Berlin, 18 November 2018.

for a Conference on the Future of Europe[128]—as will be explained in depth in Chapter 6.

4.2 The Development of EU Common Security and Defence Policy

If Brexit represented the context in which the EU27 started reflecting on their future, it also constituted the background within which the EU27 launched new policy initiatives, which were effectively rendered possible by the decision of the UK to leave the EU. In particular, following the Brexit referendum—and also in light of the changing geo-political environment, with the deterioration of transatlantic relations since the election of Donald Trump as President of the United States (US)[129]—the EU took unprecedented steps forward in the field of common foreign, security, and defence policies (CFSDPs), which had been until then repeatedly vetoed by the UK.[130] In fact, the UK had traditionally privileged its special relations with the US, and favoured action within the North Atlantic Treaty Organization (NATO), and therefore opposed earlier efforts by the EU to strengthen its military capacity and strategic autonomy. Yet, following the Brexit referendum the UK refrained from blocking the EU27 from moving forward in this field.[131]

In particular, under French leadership, on 23 June 2017 the European Council outlined a plan for further development of CFSDP, and—while reaffirming the importance of the transatlantic alliance and cooperation with NATO—endorsed greater EU integration in defence, including by agreeing for the first time ever on the need to launch the Permanent Structured Cooperation (PESCO), as allowed by Article 42(6) TEU.[132] On this basis, in December 2017 the Council authorized the activation

---

[128] French President Emmanuel Macron, Letter, 4 March 2019 https://www.elysee.fr/es/emmanuel-macron/2019/03/04/pour-une-renaissance-europeenne.fr.

[129] See also High Representative of the EU for Foreign Affairs and Security Policy, 'Shared Vision, Common Action: A Stronger Europe, A Global Strategy for the EU Foreign & Security Policy', June 2016.

[130] See Sven Biscop, 'The UK and European Defence: Leading or Leaving?' (2012) 88 *International Affairs* 1297.

[131] See further Federico Fabbrini, 'Do NATO Obligations Trump European Budgetary Constraints' (2018) 9 *Harvard National Security Journal* 121.

[132] See European Council Conclusions, 22–23 June 2017, EUCO 8/17.

of PESCO,[133] and in March 2018 it gave its blessing to the first operational projects.[134] Admittedly, it remains to be seen whether PESCO—which only involves 25 EU Member States, as Denmark and Malta have so far decided to remain outside it—will truly result in the more binding commitments foreseen in Protocol 10. In fact, shortly after the establishment of PESCO France launched a European Intervention Initiative, which invited in a more ambitious security cooperation only a selected group of 10 Member States sharing a similar security strategy.[135] Nevertheless, PESCO combined with other recent initiatives—including the Commission's roll-out of a European Defence Fund,[136] the Council's establishment of an operational planning and conduct capability infrastructure designed to oversee common security and defence policy missions and operations,[137] and the EP call for a real Defence Union[138]—testifies to the growing ambition of the EU in CFSDP after Brexit.[139]

In conclusion, during the time of the Brexit negotiations, the EU turned progressively towards a debate on the future of Europe at 27 Member States. As has been pointed out, this proved that there is still life in the EU following the Brexit referendum,[140] and that the project of European integration would continue to move forward regardless of the decision by the UK to leave the EU. In fact—while the debate on the future of Europe was admittedly more rhetoric than reality—the EU27 also took some concrete steps to develop EU policy areas that had traditionally languished when the UK was a Member State, notably CFSDPs, PESCO, and military cooperation. Nevertheless, despite Brexit other challenges continued to

---

[133] Council Decision (CFSP) 2017/2315 of 11 December 2017 establishing permanent structured cooperation (PESCO) and determining the list of participating Member States, OJ 2017 L 331/57.

[134] Council Decision (CFSP) 2018/340 of 6 March 2018 establishing the list of projects to be developed under PESCO, OJ 2018 L 65/24.

[135] In fact, see also French Minister of Defence Florence Parly, speech at the European Council on Foreign Relations, Paris, 28 May 2018 (launching the European Intervention Initiative).

[136] European Commission Communication, 'Launching the European Defence Fund', 7 June 2016, COM(2017) 295 final.

[137] Council of the EU conclusions, 'On Progress in Implementing the EU Global Strategy in the Area of Security and Defence, Annex: Concept Note: Operational Planning and Conduct Capabilities for CSDP Missions and Operations', 6 March 2017, Doc. 110/17.

[138] European Parliament resolution of 22 November 2016 on the European Defence Union, P8_TA(2016)0435.

[139] See also European Commission reflection paper on 'The Future of European Defence', 7 June 2017, COM(2017) 315 final.

[140] Caroline de Gruyter, 'There Is Life for the EU After Brexit', Carnegie Europe, 23 March 2018.

characterize, and complicate, the EU reflection and reform process—as will be pointed out in depth in Chapter 4.

5. Conclusion

This chapter has examined the EU during Brexit. The EU institutions and the remaining Member States reacted as one to the decision of the UK to leave the EU, and consistently maintained their united stance during the course of the Brexit negotiations. Nevertheless, the remarkable unity of the EU vis-à-vis the UK, and the EU's successes in securing its objectives throughout the withdrawal negotiations, cannot obfuscate the fact that Brexit absorbed significant energies, as the EU had to invest time to prepare for a possible 'hard Brexit'—and then deal with the possibility of a 'no Brexit', with the European Council considering three subsequent requests by the UK to extend its EU membership, and delay withdrawal. The fact that Brexit continued to occupy an important space in the EU agenda during the almost 44 months from the referendum to the withdrawal demonstrated therefore that the UK vote to leave the EU did not free the EU institutions and the Member States of the long-standing British question.

Yet, as the chapter has emphasized, Brexit also served as the background for the emergence of the EU27—and in that format for the launch of new constitutional debates and policy developments. Meeting at 27, without the UK, the EU Member States acknowledged that Brexit required a reflection process on the future of Europe. Moreover, they took advantage of the decision by the UK to leave the EU to push forward integration in areas such as that of security and military cooperation, where traditionally EU initiatives had been thwarted by the UK. Ultimately, the debate on the future of Europe did not move from rhetoric to reality during the time of the withdrawal negotiations. In fact, as will be shown in Chapter 4, during this period the EU27 suffered too many other crises which challenged their unity and resolve. Nevertheless, the opening of a debate on the future of Europe and the embryonic operationalization of new policy initiatives have underscored the EU's awareness during Brexit of the need to react properly to such an historical development.

3

The EU because of Brexit

Transitional Institutional Issues

1. Introduction

The withdrawal of the United Kingdom (UK) from the European Union (EU) was anything but a smooth process. While Article 50 Treaty on European Union (TEU) had settled a question which until then had remained unanswered[1]—explicitly allowing a Member State to withdraw from what is arguably the most advanced regional integration organization in the world—Brexit proved beyond doubt how difficult it is practically to leave the EU. In fact, the challenges faced by the UK—which, by being the Member State already with the most opt-outs from EU policies[2] was arguably the one with the easiest pathway out of the EU—should probably discourage any other Member State from walking the same road. Yet, the difficulty of leaving the EU did not create problems only for the UK. On the contrary, the EU also had issues because of Brexit. The purpose of this chapter is to examine specifically the transitional issues that Brexit posed for the EU's functioning and funding.

As the chapter argues, Brexit created a series of unprecedented transitional challenges for the EU's functioning. In particular, these resulted from the requests by the UK to extend its EU membership, delaying the exit day beyond the initially foreseen date of 29 March 2020.[3] In fact, in 2019, extension—which, as explained in Chapter 2, is a facility explicitly embedded in Article 50(3) TEU, allowing the European Council in agreement with the withdrawing state to postpone exit—emerged

---

[1] See Joseph H. H. Weiler, 'Alternatives to Withdrawal from an International Organization: The Case of the European Economic Community' (1985) 20 *Israel Law Review* 282.

[2] See Protocol No 15, Protocol No 20, Protocol No 30.

[3] See further Federico Fabbrini & Rebecca Schmidt, 'The Extensions' in Federico Fabbrini (ed), *The Law & Politics of Brexit: Volume II: The Withdrawal Agreement* (OUP 2020), 66.

Brexit and the Future of the European Union. Federico Fabbrini, Oxford University Press (2020). © Federico Fabbrini. DOI: 10.1093/oso/9780198871262.003.0003

as a palatable tool for the UK to avoid a 'hard Brexit'. As a result, then UK Prime Minister Theresa May, and subsequently UK Prime Minister Boris Johnson asked the European Council for three subsequent extensions, and the UK eventually left the EU only on 31 January 2020. Yet, the extensions caused serious *pro tempore* problems for the EU institutions, particularly the European Parliament (EP), but also the European Commission and the Council of the EU, which were provisionally forced to alter their composition and their working methods because of Brexit.

At the same time, Brexit also created another set of transitional challenges for the EU's funding—this time not connected to any UK extension of its EU membership, but simply to the fact that the UK withdrawal complicated negotiations for the next EU budget, the multi-annual financial framework (MFF). In fact, despite the spirit and the letter of the EU treaties, the MFF today is mostly funded by state transfers—and, despite its rebate, the UK was a net payer into the EU budget. As a result, by depriving the EU budget of the sizeable UK contribution, Brexit posed short-term problems for the next MFF 2021–2027, raising difficult questions whether to increase revenues or cut spending. Hence, because of Brexit, the EU27 were forced into tough negotiations on how to restructure the budget for a post-Brexit EU—which ended in stalemate, although these talks were later overtaken by further events, which will be analysed in Chapters 4 and 5.

As such, this chapter is structured as follows. Section 2 examines in detail the transitional implications of Brexit and the Article 50 TEU extension on the EP, analysing both the outlook of the institution and the outcome of its electoral process. To this end, the section sheds light on the changing composition of the EP owing to the participation of the UK in the EP elections, and discusses the changing balance of power in the EP, and its relationship with the Commission following first the UK presence and then the UK exit from the EU. Section 3 surveys the transitional implications of Brexit, and the delayed UK withdrawal, for the Commission and the Council of the EU. Section 4 considers the transitional implications of Brexit for the EU budget, explaining the existing mechanisms to fund the EU, and the challenges that the UK's withdrawal posed for the negotiations on the next MFF 2021–2027. Section 5 concludes.

2. The European Parliament

Brexit—or rather, the delay thereof—had significant transitional consequences for the 9th EP (2019–2024). While the UK government had notified its intention to leave the EU in March 2017 also to ensure that it would be outside the EU before the next EP elections scheduled in spring 2019 the requests for an extension of membership under Article 50(3) TEU upended that plan. In fact—as mentioned in Chapter 2—the European Council conditioned its second decision to extend the period under Article 50(3) TEU precisely on the UK taking part in the forthcoming EP elections.[4] As a result, eligible voters were called to the polls in the UK to elect the EP on 23 May 2019.[5] However, while the EP had experienced provisional alterations before then,[6] the continuing presence of the UK in the EU produced an unprecedented *pro tempore* change for the EP, with legal and political implications for both its composition and its electoral balance of powers.

2.1 The Outlook: European Parliament Composition

To begin with, as Rebecca Schmidt and I explained, the Brexit extension created a legal riddle for the composition of the 9th EP (2019–2024).[7] Pursuant to Article 14(2) TEU, the EP shall consist of a maximum of 750 members plus the President, so a total of 751 Members of the EP (MEPs). EP seats are allocated among the Member States according to the principle of degressive proportionality, with a minimum threshold for each Member State of six seats, and a maximum of 96 seats.[8] As Article 14(2) TEU clarifies, the specific allocation of EP seats in the various Member

---

[4] See European Council Decision (EU) 2019/584 taken in agreement with the United Kingdom of 11 April 2019 extending the period under Article 50(3) TEU, OJ 2019 L 101/1.

[5] See European Parliamentary Elections (Appointed Day of Poll) Order 2019 (UK).

[6] Indeed, transitional issues emerged for the EP during each enlargement of the EU, as well as following the entry into force of the Treaty of Lisbon six months after the EP elections in 2009. See further Federico Fabbrini, 'La composizione del Parlamento Europeo dopo il Trattato di Lisbona' (2011) 3 *Rivista Trimestrale di Diritto Pubblico* 859.

[7] See Federico Fabbrini & Rebecca Schmidt, 'The Composition of the European Parliament in Brexit Times: Changes and Challenges' (2019) 44 *European Law Review* 710.

[8] See further Federico Fabbrini, 'Representation in the European Parliament: of False Problems and Real Challenges' (2015) 75 *Zeitschrift für ausländisches öffentliches Recht und Völkerrecht* 823.

States is determined in a European Council decision, 'adopted by unanimity, on the initiative of the [EP] and with its consent'. De facto, then,
the European Council decision must be ratified domestically by all
Member States, since national legislation has to be put in place to regulate
the specific modalities for electing the number of MEPs assigned to each
Member State.[9] Historically, the apportionment of EP seats has been a
contentious inter-state issue, as national governments consider it a proxy
for the status of their countries.[10] In fact, elsewhere I had anticipated that
the composition of the EP following Brexit would raise the stakes in the
negotiation[11]—particularly considering that the UK held in the 8th EP
(2014–2019) 73 seats: the third largest delegation, after Germany and
France, and on a par with Italy.[12]

Following the notification by the UK of its intention to withdraw from
the EU, on 28 June 2018 the European Council adopted, on the initiative
of the EP and with its consent, a new decision on the composition of the
EP for the 9th EP.[13] Taking stock of Brexit—and therefore, of the reduction of the total EU population—the decision lowered the overall number
of MEPs from 751 to 705. At the same time, appeasing requests by several countries, it reallocated 27 of the 73 seats previously assigned to the
UK to 14 other EU Member States, in order to better fulfil the criteria of
degressive proportionality.[14] Thus, an extra one to five seats were redis-
tributed among Member States for the 9th EP term—with notably two
additional EP seats being given to Ireland owing to the fact that a high
number of citizens in Northern Ireland are also Irish citizens pursuant to

---

[9] EU law does not set a uniform procedure for the elections of MEPs, which is regulated by
national law, on the basis of common principles enshrined in the Act concerning the election
of the members of the European Parliament by direct universal suffrage, annexed to Council
Decision 76/787/ECSC, EEC, Euratom of 20 September 1976, as amended—lastly—by Council
Decision (EU, Euratom) 2018/994 of 13 July 2018 amending the Act concerning the election
of the members of the European Parliament by direct universal suffrage, annexed to Council
Decision 76/787/ECSC, EEC, Euratom of 20 September 1976, OJ 2018 L 178/1.

[10] See Jonathan Rodden, 'Strength in Numbers? Representation and Redistribution in the
European Union' (2002) 3 *European Union Politics* 151.

[11] See Federico Fabbrini, 'Brexit and EU Treaty Reform' in Federico Fabbrini (ed), *The Law &
Politics of Brexit* (OUP 2017), 267, 273.

[12] See European Council Decision of 28 June 2013 establishing the composition of the
European Parliament, 2013/312/EU, OJ 2013 L 181/57, Art. 3.

[13] European Council Decision (EU) 2018/937 of 28 June 2018 establishing the composition of
the European Parliament, OJ 2018 L 165I.

[14] See also Leonard Besselink et al, 'The impact of the UK's withdrawal on the institutional
set-up and political dynamics within the EU', study commissioned by the European Parliament
Constitutional Affairs Committee, April 2019.

the Belfast/Good Friday Agreement, and therefore entitled to continuing representation after Brexit.[15] This led to a reapportionment of seats, on the basis of the formula reported in Table 3.1.

Nevertheless, the 2018 European Council decision on the new composition of the EP also envisioned a safeguard clause. In anticipation of a (possible, although then unlikely) scenario where the UK were to remain a Member State of the EU at the time of the May 2019 EP elections, Article 3(2) of European Council Decision (EU) 2018/937 stated that:

> in the event that the United Kingdom is still a Member State of the Union at the beginning of the 2019-2024 parliamentary term, the number of representatives in the European Parliament per Member State taking up office shall be the one provided for in Article 3 of the European Council Decision 2013/312/EU until the withdrawal of the United Kingdom from the Union becomes legally effective.[16]

Moreover, that same provision foresaw that, '[o]nce the United Kingdom's withdrawal from the Union becomes legally effective, the number of representatives in the European Parliament elected in each Member State shall be the one provided' by the new allocation criteria, with the consequence that: 'All representatives in the European Parliament who fill the additional seats resulting from the difference between the number of seats allocated in the first and second subparagraphs shall take up their seats in the European Parliament at the same time'.[17]

The fact that the UK was still a Member State of the EU at the time of the May 2019 EP elections therefore had immediate implications for the incoming 9th EP (2019–2024) because this required as a necessity the UK to participate in the vote,[18] and therefore the old allocations of seats decided for the 8th EP term (2014–2019)[19] to continue, scrapping at the last minute the new seat allocation envisioned for a post-Brexit era. This

---

[15] See European Parliament resolution of 7 February 2018 on the composition of the European Parliament, P8_TA(2018)0029, para 8 (recalling that 'under the Good Friday Agreement, the people of Northern Ireland have an inherent right to hold British or Irish citizenship, or both, and by virtue of the right to Irish citizenship, to citizenship of the Union as well').

[16] European Council Decision (EU) 2018/937, Art. 3(2).

[17] Ibid.

[18] European Council Decision (EU) 2019/584, recital 10.

[19] European Council Decision 2013/312/EU.

Table 3.1: Apportionment of EP seats and pre/post-Brexit variation

Member State	MEPs 2014–2019	MEP 2019–2024 (after Brexit)	Variation
Belgium	21	21	
Bulgaria	17	17	
Czech Republic	21	21	
Denmark	13	14	+1
Germany	96	96	
Estonia	6	7	+1
Ireland	11	13	+2
Greece	21	21	
Spain	54	59	+5
France	74	79	+5
Croatia	11	12	+1
Italy	73	76	+3
Cyprus	6	6	
Latvia	8	8	
Lithuania	11	11	
Luxembourg	6	6	
Hungary	21	21	
Malta	6	6	
Netherlands	26	29	+3
Austria	18	19	+1
Poland	51	52	+1
Portugal	21	21	
Romania	32	33	+1
Slovenia	8	8	
Slovakia	13	14	+1
Finland	13	14	+1
Sweden	20	21	+1
UK	73	0	–73
Total	751	705	

created two unprecedented situations: on the one hand, the Brexit extension produced a suspensive condition for the extra 27 MEPs elected in 14
Member States—who were voted by citizens in the election but could not
take up their seats until Brexit happened; and, on the other hand, it also

produced a resolutive condition for the 73 UK-elected MEPs who joined the 9th EP but were forced to leave it—when Brexit eventually happened, on 31 January 2020. Both these situations raised novel legal issues.

On the one hand, the Brexit extension meant that 27 MEPs elected in 14 Member States were put 'in waiting'—since they were voted into office but could take up their mandates only eight months after the elections, following the formal withdrawal of the UK from the EU. While legislation rushed through at the national level just before the EP elections regulated the situation properly—for instance, specifying the conditions upon which such candidates would be regarded as elected,[20] and clarifying they would not acquire the formal status of MEPs, with the connected privileges and immunities, until after Brexit[21]—the extension of UK membership in the EU under Article 50(3) TEU generated an unprecedented suspensive condition on the EU system of democratic representation. In a first, the materialization of the people's vote was subject to an external condition—the UK's withdrawal from the EU—raising difficult questions with regard to the principle of representative democracy enshrined in Article 13 TEU.

On the other hand, the Brexit extension also meant that 73 MEPs elected in the UK took up their mandates *pro tempore*, being forced to leave their seat eight months later, when Brexit happened. As I had argued in a report commissioned by the EP Constitutional Affairs (AFCO) Committee,[22] serious legal questions arose whether requiring MEPs elected in the UK, who had fully acquired their status, to leave the EP after Brexit was compatible with EU constitutional law—including the fact that according to Article 14 TEU the MEPs represent EU citizens, not Member States, and that they serve a five-year fixed term. After all, the European Court of Justice (ECJ) recently held that 'a person who has been officially declared elected to the European Parliament must be

---

[20] See e.g. European Parliament Elections (Amendment) Act 2019, s 6j (Ir.) (stating that the extra MEPs 'shall not take up their seats in the European Parliament until such time as a date has been specified by the Parliament for the taking up of such seats').

[21] See Loi n° 2019-487 du 22 mai 2019 relative à l'entrée en fonction des représentants au Parlement européen élus en France aux élections de 2019, JORF n°0119 du 23 mai 2019, Art. unique (Fr.) (stating that '[c]es candidats prennent leur fonction de représentants au Parlement européen à compter de la date du retrait du Royaume-Uni de l'Union européenne').

[22] Federico Fabbrini, 'The Institutional Consequences of a "Hard Brexit"', study commissioned by the European Parliament Constitutional Affairs Committee, May 2018.

regarded as having acquired, as a result of this and from that time, the status of Member of that institution' and the connected privileges and immunities.[23] At the same time, considering that several of the UK-elected MEPs were either dual nationals or actually not British citizens at all,[24] it seemed hard to justify that they would be forced to vacate their seats on nationality grounds.

Ultimately, however, the withdrawal of the UK from the EU produced the change in the composition of the EP envisioned in the European Council decision on the composition of the EP[25]—and indeed reiterated in subsequent documents.[26] On the one hand, the 73 UK-elected MEPs left the EP on 31 January 2020—with much musical fanfare,[27] but with little legal resistance. On the other hand, the 27 MEPs 'in waiting' elected in 14 other EU Member States took up their seats on 1 February 2020.[28] Hence, the legal outlook of the 9th EP (2014–2019) changed while the term was in progress, with an overall shrinking of the institution from 751 members to 705—just over eight months after EU citizens had been called to the polls. Yet, the transitional modification in the composition of the EP also had consequences for the political outlook of the EP, its internal balance of powers, and its relations with the other EU institutions.[29]

---

[23] Case C-502/19 *Criminal proceedings against Oriol Junqueras Vies*, EU:C:2019:1115, para 81.

[24] See also 'The Brexit Vote: Here are all the MEPs elected for Britain and Northern Ireland', *The Journal*, 28 May 2019 (reporting the names of all the 73 MEPs elected in Great Britain and Northern Ireland, and indicating that among others Henrik Overgaard-Nielsen (Brexit Party) has dual British and Danish citizenship; Irina Von Wiese (Lib Dems) has British and German citizenship; Christian Allard (SNP) has British and French citizenship; and Martina Anderson (Sinn Fein) has only Irish (not British) citizenship).

[25] European Council Decision (EU) 2018/937.

[26] See also European Council Decision (EU) 2019/584 recital 11 (stating that '[t]he ongoing mandates of members of institutions, bodies, offices and agencies of the Union nominated, appointed or elected in relation to the United Kingdom's membership of the Union will end as soon as the Treaties cease to apply to the United Kingdom, i.e. on the date of the withdrawal.')

[27] See Eszter Zalan, 'EU Parliament bids tearful farewell to British MEPs', *EuObserver*, 30 January 2020.

[28] See European Parliament press release, 'Redistribution of seats in the European Parliament After Brexit', 31 January 2020.

[29] See also European Parliament resolution of 12 February 2019 on the implementation of the Treaty provisions on Parliament's power of political control over the Commission, P8_TA(2019)0078, para 1 (recalling that 'the accountability of the Commission to Parliament is an underpinning principle of the functioning of the EU and of internal democratic control') and European Commission recommendation (EU) 2018/234 of 14 February 2018 on enhancing the European nature and efficient conduct of the 2019 elections to the European Parliament, OJ 2018 L 45/40.

2.2 The Outcome: European Parliament Elections

The elections for the 9th EP were in many ways a watershed.[30] For the first time since the introduction of direct universal suffrage for the EP in 1979, electoral participation to the vote rose to 51%, experiencing a 25-year high, with an increase of almost 10% compared to 2014.[31] This confirmed the growing interest for EU politics but also a growing polarization in public attitudes towards the EU—a sentiment that had been captured by the Spring 2019 Eurobarometer[32] and exposed during the electoral campaign. While French President Emmanuel Macron took up the leadership of the pro-European forces, addressing an open letter to all European citizens (written in the 22 official languages of the EU) *pour une renaissance européenne*,[33] sovereigntist forces made clear their ambition to take control of the EU machine and fundamentally weaken the system from within.[34] During spring 2019, tensions between pro- and anti-EU forces soured to the point that they spilled over from the political to the diplomatic realm: in an unprecedented move, France recalled its ambassador from Italy after the then Italian Deputy Prime Minister Luigi Di Maio, leader of the *Movimento 5 Stelle*, met the self-proclaimed mastermind of the *Gilet Jaunes* movement, which had openly suggested staging a military *coup d'état* against French President Macron.[35]

The outcome of the vote for the 9th EP, which took place between 23 and 26 May 2019, crystallized the competition between alternative visions for Europe.[36] In the end, in the second largest democratic exercise in the world (after India), pro-European parties managed overall to cling on to control the EP. In the parliamentary term that opened on

---

[30] See 2019 European elections result https://www.election-results.eu/.

[31] See also European Council President Donald Tusk, remarks after the informal dinner of heads of state and government, 28 May 2019, 404/19 (stating that the leaders 'are very happy about the turnout which is the highest in 25 years') and European Commission Communication 'Report on the 2019 elections of the European Parliament', 19 June 2020, COM(2020) 252 final.

[32] Eurobarometer Spring 2019, 25 April 2019.

[33] French President Emmanuel Macron, Letter, 4 March 2019 https://www.elysee.fr/es/emmanuel-macron/2019/03/04/pour-une-renaissance-europeenne.fr.

[34] See Barbara Fiammeri, 'Salvini da Kaczyński: al via il "progetto" sovranista in UE', *Il Sole 24 Ore*, 9 January 2019.

[35] See 'La France rappelle son ambassadeur en Italie à la suite "d'attaques sans précédent"', *Le Monde*, 7 February 2019.

[36] See European Parliamentary Research Service, Size of Political Groups in the EP at a Glance, Infographic, 2 July 2019.

2 July 2019, with the EP composition at 751 members, pro-EU forces were in clear majority.[37] This was facilitated by the impressive gains for liberal-democratic parties and the Greens, which increased their EP seats, respectively, from 67 to 105, and from 50 to 69. In fact, the liberal-democratic bloc—historically known as the Alliance of Liberals and Democrats for Europe (ALDE)—rebranded itself as the Renew Europe group, marking its role as a strong pro-integration force in the EP. Nevertheless, for the first time since 1979, the two political families which had traditionally dominated the EP—the European People's Party (EPP) and the Socialists & Democrats (S&D)—lost their cumulative majority, winning a total of 'only' 182 and 154 EP seats respectively. Moreover, the vote still strengthened the anti-European factions within the EP, with the European Conservatives & Reformists (ERC), the populists and the nationalists holding 63, 43, and 73 EP seats apiece. In fact, while the populists failed to reach the minimal requirement to form a group, and thus ended up gathering as non-affiliated members, the 73-seat strong main sovereigntist force in the EP established a new parliamentary group and named it Identity & Democracy, suggesting a strong polarization in the 9th EP term.[38]

Nevertheless, the election also exposed relevant national variation. In particular, in Hungary and Poland the governing right-wing parties, *Fidesz* and *PiS*, topped the polls with 53% and 45% of the vote respectively, while in Italy the *Lega*, a nationalist party led by the then fire-brand Deputy Prime Minister Matteo Salvini won the national vote with 34% support and 28 EP seats. By contrast, S&D parties performed well in Portugal, the Netherlands, and Denmark, and the EPP won the elections in Ireland, Greece, and Germany, where *Die Grünen* emerged as the biggest electoral surprise, coming in second place with 20% of the vote. Moreover, while in France President Macron's movement *La République En Marche* trailed Marine Le Pen's *Rassemblement nationale*, pro-European forces overall secured a higher number of EP seats, thanks again to a surprising performance by the environmentalist party *Europe Ecologie Les Verts*, which secured 13% of the vote. In Spain, instead, a

---

[37] Corinne Deloy, 'La progression des populistes est contenue par la hausse des libéraux et des écologistes aux élections européennes', Fondation Robert Schuman, June 2019.

[38] See generally also Marlene Wind, *The Tribalization of Europe* (Wiley 2020).

special problem arose owing to the election of three Catalan leaders who were either under arrest or subject to prosecution in connection with the botched 2017 Catalan independence referendum: one of them, Oriol Junqeras, challenged the impossibility of joining the EP before the ECJ, which ruled that he enjoyed parliamentary immunity as of his election,[39] but the Spanish Tribunal Supremo held that his prior criminal conviction made him ineligible to hold office[40]—with the consequence that a seat in the 751-members EP remained vacant.[41]

At the same time, the EP elections—in which the UK participated against all odds—turned into a political earthquake for the UK too, confirming a major restructuring of its party system. With both Labour and the Conservatives uncertain even whether to run an electoral campaign, the triumph at the ballot box was for the newly founded, single-issue Brexit Party of Nigel Farage: running on a simple Leave platform, the Brexit Party topped the national competition, drawing almost 32% of the national vote and securing for itself 29 out of 73 UK seats in the EP (where, however, it ended joining the non-affiliated group, with limited internal influence). Nevertheless, the EP elections also showed an excellent performance for parties which explicitly embraced a Remain position, in particular the Liberal Democrats (Lib Dems) and the Greens, as well as the Scottish National Party and Plaid Cymru: with 16, seven, four, and one EP seats each, all these forces improved their performance compared to the 2014 EP elections. Instead, the vote was a bloodbath for Labour—and particularly for the Conservatives. While Labour payed for its indecisive position on Europe, drawing just 14% of the vote, slicing in half its contingent at the EP (from 20 to 10 EP seats) and ending up in third position in the ranking, the Conservative Party ended up in fifth place, with a meagre 9% of the national votes, and four EP seats (15 seats fewer than in 2014).

---

[39] Case C-502/19 *Criminal proceedings against Oriol Junqueras Vies* (n 23).

[40] Tribunal Supremo, Sala de lo Penal, causa especial num. 20907/2017, judgment of 9 January 2020.

[41] See European Parliament minutes, Composition of the European Parliament, 13 January 2020 (taking note of the judgments of the ECJ and of the Spanish Tribunal Supremo and declaring the seat of Mr Junqueras vacant owing to his criminal conviction, while instead declaring the two other Catalan leaders full MEPs with retroactive effect as of 2 July 2019). Mr Oriol Junqueras subsequently challenged the determination of the EP. See Case T-24/20 *Junqueras i Vies v Parliament*, pending.

The outcome of the EP elections created significant challenges for the start of the new EU institutional cycle, and notably for the choice of the next European Commission President.[42] Pursuant to Article 17(7) TEU '[t]aking into account the elections of the European Parliament ... the European Council, acting by a qualified majority, shall propose to the European Parliament a candidate for President of the Commission. This candidate shall be elected by the European Parliament by a majority of its component members'; the EP scrutinizes the candidates put forward by the Member States for the role of Commissioners; and '[t]he President, the High Representative of the Union for Foreign Affairs and Security Policy and the other members of the Commission shall be subject as a body to a vote of consent by the European Parliament'. On the one hand, given the fragmentation resulting from the EP elections, two summits on 20 June 2019[43] and on 1 July 2019[44] were not enough for heads of state and government to reach a compromise on the nominees for the top EU jobs. On the other hand, given the participation of the UK in the EP elections, UK-elected MEPs came to play a highly relevant role in the formation of the new Commission.

Ultimately, the European Council decided to ditch the Spitzenkandidaten process—which had been experimented in 2014, whereby the post of European Commission President would be assigned to the lead candidate of the parties winning more EP seats[45]—and instead nominated an outsider to do the job: German Defence Minister Ursula von der Leyen.[46] When the Commission President-nominee stood before the EP on 16 July 2019, however, she was elected with a margin of only nine votes: 383 votes in favour, 327 against, and 22 abstaining, with the threshold needed to be elected being 374 votes.[47] Crucially, this majority—encompassing the EPP and Renew Europe but only part

---

[42] See also Jan-Herman Reestman & Leonard Besselink, Editorial, 'Spitzenkandidaten and the European Union's System of Government' (2019) 15 European Constitutional Law Review 609.

[43] See European Council President Donald Tusk, statement, 20 June 2019.

[44] See European Council President Donald Tusk, statement, 1 July 2019.

[45] See further Federico Fabbrini et al (eds), What Form of Government for the EU and the Eurozone? (Hart Publishing 2015).

[46] See European Council Conclusions, 2 July 2019, EUCO 18/19 (simultaneously electing Charles Michel next European Council President, and identifying Christine Lagarde as next European Central Bank President).

[47] See European Parliament press release, 'European Parliament Elects Ursula von der Leyen as First Female Commission President', 16 July 2019.

of the S&D and others—also included the votes of UK-elected MEPs.[48] Although the ballot was secret, it was reported that the 16 Lib Dem MEPs, affiliated to the new Renew Europe group, as well as the 10 Labour and four Conservative MEPs, affiliated respectively to the S&D and the ECR groups in the EP, voted for President-candidate Von der Leyen and thus were instrumental in securing her majority.[49]

As a result, the transitional change in the composition of the EP owing to the extension of the UK's membership of the EU, and eventually the UK's withdrawal from the EU, also has the potential to alter the political relation of confidence between the EP and the new Commission. In fact, the exit of the 73 UK-elected MEPs on 31 January 2020 and the entry of 27 MEPs elected in 14 other Member States from 1 February 2020 modified the absolute size and relative weight of the EP groups. With the S&D down to 147 seats, Renew Europe to 98, and the Greens to 67, while the EPP grew in size up to 184 seats, and Identity & Democracy to 76,[50] Brexit shifted the balance of power within the EP to the right—as shown in Table 3.2. This is reflected also in the fact that Identity & Democracy overtook the Greens as the fourth largest faction in the EP.[51] While it is not clear whether this will turn the EP upside down, and threaten the political stability of the Commission, there is no doubt therefore that the transitional problems created by Brexit reverberated throughout the EU institutional system.

3. The Functioning of the EU

In fact, Brexit—or, rather, its delay, owing to the extension of Article 50(3) TEU—also had transitional complications for other EU institutions, namely the Commission and the Council.

---

[48] See further Fabbrini & Schmidt (n 7).

[49] See Joe Barnes, 'British MEPs help crown Brexit-hating von der Leyen queen of Europe', *The Express*, 17 July 2019.

[50] See European Parliamentary Research Service, Size of Political Groups in the EP, Infographic, 13 February 2020..

[51] Christine Verger, 'Le Brexit va-t-il bouleverser le Parlement européen', Notre Europe Institut Jacques Delors, 21 January 2020.

Table 3.2: Size of European Parliamentary Groups and pre/post-Brexit variation

Political Groups	Seats before Brexit (1/7/2019–31/1/2020)	Seats after Brexit (1/2/2020 onwards)	Variation
European People's Party (EPP)	182	187	+5
Socialists & Democrats (S&D)	154	147	–8
Renew Europe	108	98	–10
Greens	74	67	–7
Identity & Democracy (ID)	73	76	+3
European Conservatives & Reformists (ECR)	62	61	–1
European United Left/Nordic Green Left (GUE/NGL)	41	39	–2
Not affiliated	54	29	–25

3.1 European Commission

To begin with, the delay in the withdrawal also had implications for the composition of the Commission itself, which entered into operation on 1 December 2020[52]—one month later than originally planned, owing to rejection by the EP of several candidates for the role of Commissioner put forward by the Member States in the Council, partly on competence grounds but mostly in retaliation for the European Council's decision to abandon the Spitzenkandidaten process.[53] Pursuant to Article 17(5) TEU—as amended by a unanimous decision of the European Council,[54] adopted in the aftermath of the first Irish referendum on the Lisbon

---

[52] European Parliament Decision of 27 November 2019 electing the Commission, P9_TA(2019)0067.

[53] See David Herszenhorn et al, 'Von der Leyen Commission faces delay after French nominee's rejection', *Politico*, 10 October 2019.

[54] See European Council Decision of 22 May 2013 concerning the number of members of the European Commission 2013/272/EU, OJ 2013 L 165/98, Art. 1 (stating that '[t]he Commission shall consist of a number of members … equal to the number of Member States').

Treaty—the Commission shall consist of one national for each Member State. As such, in approving the third extension under Article 50(3) TEU therefore, the European Council required the UK 'to suggest a candidate for appointment as member of the Commission',[55] in order to make sure that the Commission would have a composition of 28 members, at least for the time being.

However, on 23 August 2019, the UK government announced that it would not nominate a UK Commissioner for the 2019–2024 term.[56] As the UK Permanent Representative to the EU Sir Tim Barrows explained in a letter to the head of the new Commission President's transition team,[57] the move was 'not intended to stop the EU appointing a new Commission',[58] and the UK 'will not object to the Council, in accordance with Article 17(7) [TEU] and in agreement with the President-elect, adopting the list of candidates for the appointment as members of the Commission and communicating that list to the European Parliament'.[59] Moreover, despite the requests by the new Commission President Von der Leyen after the third extension decision, UK Prime Minister Boris Johnson still refused to put forward the name of a Commissioner. Hence, with the new Commission due to take office on 1 December 2019, concerns emerged whether it was legally waterproof to proceed in forming a Commission of 27 when the EU still had 28 Member States. As a result, on 13 November 2019 the Commission took the unprecedented step of starting infringement proceedings against the UK.[60] Yet, on 25 November 2019 the Council appointed the Commission at 27, stating that 'although only 27 persons are proposed for appointment as Members of the Commission, the Commission is composed, in accordance with Decision 2013/272/EU,

[55] European Council Decision (EU) 2019/1810 taken in agreement with the United Kingdom of 28 October 2019 extending the period under Article 50(3)TEU, OJ 2019 L 278/I, recital 11.

[56] UK government press release, 'The UK will not nominate a new Commissioner to the EU', 23 August 2019.

[57] UK Permanent Representative to the EU Sir Tim Barrow, Letter to the Head of Transition Team (European Commission President-elect) and the Secretary General of the Council of the European Union, 23 August 2019.

[58] Ibid.

[59] Ibid.

[60] European Commission press release, 'European Commission launches infringement proceedings against the UK following its failure to name a candidate for EU Commissioner', 14 November 2019.

of a number of Members equal to the number of Member States'[61]—and the UK withdrawal from the EU on 31 January 2020 ultimately mooted the Commission's infringement case.

3.2 Council of the EU

Secondly, the Brexit extension also had implications for the Council of the EU, raising two novel issues. To begin with, the UK continued to remain a member of the Council for the extension period—posing challenges for the functionality of the institutions given the risks of disruptive behaviour from a withdrawing Member State.[62] In fact, as explained in Chapter 2, in all its extension decisions the European Council required the UK to abide by the principle of sincere cooperation, and avoid disrupting the work of the Council.[63] The concern that this could happen was anything but abstract. Jacob Rees-Mogg, a leader of the pro-Brexit camp, had openly called on the UK to be as difficult as possible if the EU were to prevent the UK from leaving,[64] and the strategy of undermining the EU from within could well have been put into action after UK Prime Minister Boris Johnson nominated him as Leader of the House Commons.[65] It was precisely to avert this threat that the European Council in accepting the request for a second extension demanded that the UK government act in a constructive and responsible manner throughout the extension period in compliance with the Treaty-based duty of sincere cooperation.[66] Yet, it was not clear whether this could be fully expected, and how it could be

---

[61] Council Decision (EU) 2019/1949 taken by common accord with the President-elect of the Commission of 25 November 2019 adopting the list of the other persons whom the Council proposes for appointment as Members of the Commission, and repealing and replacing Decision (EU) 2019/1393, OJ 2019 L 304/16, recital 3.

[62] See further Fabbrini & Schmidt (n 3).

[63] European Council Decision (EU) 2019/476 taken in agreement with the United Kingdom of 22 March 2019 extending the period under Article 50(3) TEU, OJ 2019 L 80 I/1 recital 10; European Council Conclusions, 10 April 2019, EUCO XT 20015/19, para 10; European Council Decision (EU) 2019/1810, recital 11.

[64] See Laurenz Gehrke & Ginger Hervey, 'Rees-Mogg: UK should be "as difficult as possible" with EU if Brexit delayed', *Politico*, 5 April 2019.

[65] Alistair Smout, 'UK PM Johnson appoints Rees-Mogg as leader of the House of Commons', *Reuters*, 24 July 2019.

[66] See European Council Decision (EU) 2019/584, recital 10.

enforced.[67] Nevertheless, eventually, the threat of UK disruption of the Council did not happen.

Rather, the UK increasingly carved out for itself a diminished role in the Council. Of course—as already indicated in Chapter 2—under Article 50(4) TEU, 'the member of the European Council or of the Council representing the withdrawing Member State shall not participate in the discussions of the European Council or Council or in decisions concerning it'—so effectively the UK had been excluded since 2017 from Council and European Council meetings dealing with Brexit. Moreover, the EU27 had increasingly caucused without the UK to discuss the future of Europe. However, during the extension period the UK reduced its involvement in Council work even further. On 19 August 2019, the UK government announced that it would stop attending most meetings of the Council of the EU as of 1 September 2019.[68] As explained by the UK Secretary of State for Exiting the EU Stephen Barclay, '[t]his will free up time for Ministers and their officials to get on with preparing for our departure …'.[69] Nevertheless, while the UK government indicated that this 'decision is not intended in any way to frustrate the functioning of the EU',[70] it clarified that it would continue to attend meetings of the Council of the EU, 'where the UK has a significant national interest in the outcome of discussions'[71]—listing meetings on the UK's exit, sovereignty, international relations, security, or finance as examples.

As a result, by choosing selectively whether to exercise its right to participate in Council of the EU meetings—and, correspondingly, by arranging to delegate pursuant to Article 239 Treaty on the Functioning of the European Union (TFEU) its voting rights to Finland, as the Member State then holding the six-month presidency of the Council of the EU—the UK impacted on the decision-making process in the Council. In fact, if this is seen in conjunction with the UK's unilateral decision not to exercise its

---

[67] See further Federico Fabbrini & Miguel Maduro, 'Is the EU prepared if the UK were to stay', Op-Ed, *EU News*, 10 January 2019.
[68] UK government press release, 'UK officials will stop attending most EU meetings from 1 September', 20 August 2019.
[69] Ibid.
[70] Ibid.
[71] Ibid.

right to nominate a Commissioner, the UK willy-nilly continued to influence the functioning of the EU, while protecting its 'ongoing national interest'.[72] Even though the UK remained during the extension period an EU Member State 'with full rights and obligations',[73] it effectively carved out for itself a diminished membership status, with only partial involvement in the governance of the EU. It appears that during a sizeable 10-month extension period, from 29 March 2019 until the withdrawal from the EU on 31 January 2020, the UK de facto shaped for itself a status of semi-Member State, as an antechamber towards full exit.

4. The Financing of the EU

Besides its implications on the functioning of the EU institutions, Brexit also had significant transitional consequences for the financing of the EU. These effects were not transitional in the sense that they compelled the EU to make *pro tempore* changes to its arrangements, as happened notably with the composition of the EP. In fact, the Agreement on the Withdrawal of the UK from the EU included provisions on the financial settlement, which required the UK to fulfil its budgetary obligations vis-à-vis the EU, including continuing to pay its full share for the 2020 budget (a period of time during which, in any case, the UK would be part of the internal market, thanks to the transition period).[74] Rather, Brexit posed new challenges for the preparation of the EU's next MFF 2021–2027, which started while the UK was still a Member State, and continued thereafter. Indeed, one of the reasons why the UK set its exit date initially in 2019 (and later refused to extend the transition period beyond 2020) was precisely to avoid having to participate in the EU's new MFF 2021–2027. However, because of the way in which the EU system of revenues and expenditures is structured, the UK's withdrawal from the EU posed transitional challenges for the EU's budget, which invariably arose in the MFF negotiations.

---

[72] Ibid.

[73] See European Council Decision (EU) 2019/584, recital 10.

[74] See Agreement on the withdrawal of the United Kingdom of Great Britain and Northern Ireland from the European Union and the European Atomic Energy Community, OJ 2020 L 29/07, Part V.

4.1   EU Revenues and Expenditures

The EU treaties' provisions regulating the financing of the EU set up a highly technical and complex system, which can be summarized as follows.[75] Firstly, under Article 312 TFEU, the Council, acting unanimously and with the consent of the EP shall adopt a regulation laying down the MFF of the EU: this regulation, usually adopted for a seven-year period, 'shall ensure that Union expenditure develops in an orderly manner'. Secondly, under Article 311 TFEU, the Council, acting unanimously and after consulting the EP shall adopt a decision laying down the system of own resources of the Union: this decision—which 'shall not enter into force until it is approved by the Member States in accordance with their respective constitutional requirements'—defines the *revenue* side of EU financing, and thus complements the MFF regulation which instead sets the *expenditure*. Thirdly, based on the funding prospect set in the own resources decision and in light of the expenditure plan sketched in the MFF regulation, the EP and the Council jointly adopt every year the annual budget of the EU according to Article 314 TFEU.

The rules on the financing of the EU for the MFF 2014–2020 were set in a package of legal measures adopted with difficulty at the end of the previous budget cycle.[76] In particular, on the revenue side, the EU own resources were set out in a Council decision adopted in May 2014.[77] On the expenditure side, , instead, the rules were condensed in a Council regulation adopted in December 2013, which laid out the MFF for 2014–2020.[78] Both these legal measures were the result of highly complex political negotiations. A proposal for a new own resources decision had been tabled by the Commission in 2011,[79] and it took three years to approve it in the Council, with additional time later on for parliamentary ratification in the Member States—although this applied retroactively as from 1 January

---

[75] See further Federico Fabbrini, *Economic Governance in Europe* (OUP 2016).

[76] See Luca Zamparini & Ubaldo Villani-Lubelli (eds), *Features and Challenges of the EU Budget* (Edward Elgar Publishing 2019).

[77] Council Decision of 26 May 2014 on the system of own resources of the European Union, 2014/335/EU, Euratom, OJ 2014 L 168/105.

[78] Council Regulation (EU, Euratom) No 1311/2013 of 2 December 2013 laying down the multiannual financial framework for the years 2014-2020, OJ 2013 L 347/884.

[79] See Commission proposal for a Council Decision on the system of own resources of the European Union, 29 June 2011, COM(2011) 510 final.

2014, when national ratifications were completed.[80] At the same time, negotiations for the MFF 2014–2020 broke down on several occasions, and the intervention of the European Council (in place of the Council) was necessary in order to find a compromise among the Member States.[81]

As is well known, the difficulties in negotiating the own resources decision and the MFF regulation are a result of the way in which the EU is currently funded.[82] Contrary to the High Authority of the European Carbon and Steel Community (ECSC), which was empowered to collect levies from private companies and borrow on the markets to finance itself,[83] the EU today is mostly funded by budgetary transfers from the Member States, based on their GDP, or the income derived by a harmonized value-added tax (VAT).[84] Owing to this state of affairs, the decision-making process about the EU budget has been captured by endless negotiations among the Member States regarding the precise costs and benefits that each would incur. Because no Member State is willing to transfer *its* money to the EU budget for the benefit of *other* Member States, the discussions about the EU funding have become increasingly costly and decreasingly effective—every Member State having a veto power on how much resources the EU should raise and how it should spend them.

Given this situation, I predicted that one could expect the negotiations of the new EU MFF 2021–2027 to be highly contentious after Brexit.[85] Although the UK enjoyed a famous rebate (obtained in 1984, and preserved ever since) which allowed it to pay less than it should, it still remained one of the major contributors to the EU budget: the fourth total net payer into the EU's coffers, after Germany, France, and Italy.[86] Hence, Brexit raised the question of how to handle the loss of UK contributions to the EU's budget. In principle, the EU could reduce expenditure in proportion to the UK quota—but one could anticipate that Member States

[80] See Council Decision 2014/335/EU, Euratom, Art. 11.

[81] See European Council meeting, 22–23 November 2012.

[82] See Federico Fabbrini, 'Taxing and Spending in the Eurozone' (2014) 39 *European Law Review* 155.

[83] Art. 49, ECSC Treaty.

[84] See also Alessandro D'Alfonso, 'How the EU budget is financed. The "own resources" system and the debate on its reform', European Parliament Research Service in-depth analysis, 2 June 2014, 140805REV1.

[85] See Fabbrini (n 11) 274.

[86] See European Commission, 'EU Expenditure and Revenue 2014-2020', interactive chart http://ec.europa.eu/budget/figures/interactive/index_en.cfm.

which are net beneficiaries of EU spending would not endorse such an outcome. Alternatively, Member States which are net contributors to the EU budget could increase their contributions to make up the shortfall— but again one could anticipate that countries which are already paying into the EU budget more than what they get in return would not endorse this option either. In this context, I also suggested in a study commissioned by the EP AFCO Committee that Brexit could also create an opportunity to rethink more fundamentally the system of own resources and establish new taxes to sustain a fiscal capacity.[87]

4.2 The New Budget Negotiations

As a matter of fact, Brexit generated exactly the above-mentioned conundrum, and the EU27 experienced another tense confrontation in the context of the negotiations on the new MFF. As has been pointed out, while the EU succeeded in legally binding the UK towards a financial settlement in the Withdrawal Agreement, it was forced to make stark choices on its next budget, to account for the loss of the UK's financial contributions into the EU's coffers.[88] Admittedly, clashes among Member States have always characterized EU budget negotiations. However, Brexit raised the stakes and added new complications for the EU, which materialized while the UK was still a Member State and exploded by the time it had left. This can be regarded as one of the most significant transitional changes for the EU because of Brexit—although the ultimate shape of the MFF 2021–2027 was subsequently influenced to a much greater degree by the unprecedented Covid-19 pandemic, and the responses taken to tackle it, which will be analysed in Chapters 4 and 5.

In preparation for the new MFF 2021–2027, on 2 May 2018 the European Commission put forward a draft proposal for the future EU budget,[89] and correspondingly, a proposal for the new EU own resources

---

[87] See Federico Fabbrini, 'A Fiscal Capacity for the Eurozone: Constitutional Perspectives', study commissioned by the European Parliament Constitutional Affairs Committee, February 2019.

[88] See Michele Chang, 'The Financial Settlement' in Federico Fabbrini (ed), *The Law & Politics of Brexit: Volume II: The Withdrawal Agreement* (OUP 2020), 131.

[89] European Commission proposal for a Council Regulation laying down the multiannual financial framework for the years 2021 to 2027, 2 May 2018, COM(2018) 322 final.

decision.[90] The Commission's plan sought to find a compromise between the positions of the EP[91] and France,[92] which pushed for an ambitious budget, and those of Germany, which instead endorsed a more conservative stance.[93] As such, the Commission's plan foresaw an MFF 2021–2027 worth 1.11% of EU GDP—a decrease compared to the previous MFF 2014–2020—and with a significant reallocation of resources from the traditional areas of the Common Agricultural Policy (CAP) and cohesion policy towards new priorities, including research and innovation, environmental, and digital policy, as well as foreign, security, and migration policy.[94] Moreover, taking stock of Brexit, the Commission also proposed to phase out the correction mechanisms applicable to Germany, Austria, the Netherlands, Denmark, and Sweden resulting from the UK rebate, so as to ensure greater fairness and transparency in the system.[95] Finally, the Commission also proposed to introduce a mechanism to freeze structural funds for EU Member States which failed to respect the rule of law.[96]

The Commission's new MFF package was tabled over a year before the expected withdrawal of the UK. However, the real negotiations on the budget only started after the EP elections of May 2019, and continued during the extension of the UK's membership of the EU and beyond it. In fact, the Council of the EU failed to make any progress on the MFF negotiations during the Finnish and Croatian presidencies in 2019/2020—owing to the intractable divisions among Member States. In particular, on the one hand, a group of four Nordic nations—Austria, the Netherlands, Denmark, and Sweden—which self-proclaimed themselves frugal, staunchly called for further budget cuts with a smaller

---

[90] European Commission proposal for a Council Decision on the system of own resources of the European Union, 2 May 2018, COM(2018) 325 final.

[91] See European Parliament resolution of 14 March 2018 on the next MFF: Preparing the Parliament's position on the MFF post-2020, P8_TA(2018)0075.

[92] See French government, Note des autorités françaises, 9 January 2018.

[93] See German government, Positionen der Bundesregierung zum Mehrjähri-gen Finanzrahmen der EU (MFR) post-2020, 25 January 2018.

[94] See European Commission Communication, 'A Modern Budget for a Union that Protects, Empowers and Defends: The Multiannual Financial Framework for 2021-2027', 2 May 2018, COM(2018) 321 final.

[95] See also Jörg Haas & Eulalia Rubio, 'Brexit and the EU Budget: Threat or Opportunity?', Notre Europe Institut Jacques Delors policy paper 183, 16 January 2017.

[96] European Commission proposal for a regulation of the European Parliament and the Council on the protection of the Union's budget in case of generalised deficiencies as regards the rule of law in the Member States, 2 May 2018, COM(2018) 324 final.

envelope for the traditional EU policies.[97] On the other hand, an alliance of 16 Eastern and Southern Member States caucusing as the friends of cohesion[98]—including the Visegrad (Poland, Hungary, Czechia, and Slovakia) and Baltic (Estonia, Latvia, and Lithuania) countries, Bulgaria, Romania, Croatia, Slovenia, Greece, Italy, Malta, and Portugal—insisted on maintaining proper funding for the CAP and cohesion policies, while the Eastern EU Member States also opposed the plan to introduce rule of law conditionality in the MFF. As a result, a special European Council meeting convened on 21 February 2020—exactly three weeks after the UK had left the EU—ended in a fiasco.[99] If this proved that a focus on the *juste retour* in the budget negotiations was not an exclusive feature of the time when the UK was a Member State of the EU, the difficulties of the EU27 in reaching a deal on the MFF 2021–2027 revealed the transitional legacy that Brexit posed for the EU and its financial arrangements.[100]

5. Conclusion

This chapter has analysed the EU because of Brexit. The EU's functioning was heavily affected by Brexit—and particularly by the UK extension of its EU membership, which delayed withdrawal. As a consequence of the postponement of Brexit from 29 March 2019 to 31 January 2020, all EU institutions had to face transitional changes and new challenges. Especially for the EP, this meant that the composition had to be altered during the course of the 9th term (2019–2024), with 73 MEPs elected in the UK taking up their posts for seven months, and 27 MEPs elected in 14 other EU Member States on the basis of a pre-agreed reallocation of seats only able to take up their function nine months after the EP elections. This had consequences also for the political balance of power within the EP, and its relationship of confidence with the Commission. Yet the transitional problems faced by the EP mirrored those of the Council of the

---

[97] See Austrian Chancellor Sebastian Kurz, 'The "Frugal Four" Advocate a Responsible EU Budget', Op-Ed, *Financial Times*, 16 February 2020.

[98] Mateusz Morawiecki, 'Polish PM: EU budget is about more than arithmetic', Op-Ed, *Financial Times*, 19 February 2020.

[99] See European Council President Charles Michel, remarks, 21 February 2020.

[100] See also Peter Becker, 'A New Budget for the EU: Negotiations on the Multiannual Financial Framework 2021-2027', Stiftung Wissenschaft und Politik research paper 11, August 2019.

EU, and the Commission itself, which also started infringement proceedings against the UK for failure to appoint a commissioner.

At the same time, because of Brexit the EU also faced other transitional difficulties with regard to the new MFF. While these did not result from the UK extension of its EU membership, Brexit still complicated things for the EU, as it left a significant gap in the EU budget, and forced the EU27 into complicated negotiations regarding the next MFF 2021–2027. Indeed, although EU budget talks have always been difficult because of the way in which the EU is currently funded, the UK's withdrawal aggravated in the short term the clash between Member States negotiating how to restructure the budget, with net payers seeking to cut expenditure and net beneficiaries seeking to increase revenues. In fact, budget negotiations on the MFF 2021–2027, which commenced during the UK's membership of the EU, ended in a fiasco in February 2020, just three weeks after Brexit, proving both the legacy of the UK's withdrawal and the ongoing shortcomings of the EU's governance system.

4

The EU besides Brexit

Crises Governance

1. Introduction

One of the most remarkable features of the withdrawal negotiations has been the unity of the European Union (EU) vis-à-vis the United Kingdom (UK). During Brexit, the EU27 never divided in their dealings with the UK. On the contrary, as Irish Taoiseach Leo Varadkar gratefully noted, the EU27 proved able to stick together and jointly defend their common interests, including those of the smaller Member States.[1] However, one would be mistaken in believing that the unity of the EU27 vis-à-vis the UK reflects a generally high level of harmony within the EU. In fact, in the last decade the EU institutions and Member States have faced an increasing number of crises, which have profoundly challenged their unity and resolve. The purpose of this chapter is to examine the EU besides Brexit, exposing the powerful centrifugal pressures at play within the EU, and explaining the EU's challenges in crises governance in light of competing visions of integration.

As the chapter argues, in addition to Brexit, the EU has recently experienced a plurality of other crises. Some of these crises—including the euro-crisis, the migration crisis, and the rule of law crisis—predated Brexit. But others—including the debate on enlargement and climate change—have followed it. In fact, the battery of crises afflicting the EU reached its climax just months after the UK's withdrawal, with the explosion of the coronavirus, a new, severe acute respiratory syndrome known also by its medical acronym Covid-19, which has resulted in the largest pandemic the world has experienced,

---

[1] See Irish Taoiseach Leo Varadkar, 'Thank you to the People of Europe', Op-Ed, *Irish Times*, 31 January 2020.

Brexit and the Future of the European Union. Federico Fabbrini, Oxford University Press (2020). © Federico Fabbrini. DOI: 10.1093/oso/9780198871262.003.0004

at least since the 1918 Spanish influenza. Originally emerging in China in December 2019, the virus slowly but steadily spread across the globe, reaching Europe in February 2020. With its tragic death toll, Covid-19 prompted unprecedented responses by public authorities, and proved to be both a dramatic health and a devastating socioeconomic crisis for the EU27.

The EU struggled to govern these crises successfully. In fact, both the old and the new crises exposed deep divisions among the EU27 and brought competing visions of the project of European integration to the surface. In particular, as this chapter claims, three alternative ideas of what the EU is and ought to be are increasingly taking shape: a first that sees the EU as a polity, which requires solidarity and a communion of efforts towards a shared destiny; a second that sees the EU as a market, designed to enhance wealth through commerce, but with as limited redistribution as possible; and a third which instead sees the EU as a vehicle to entrench state authoritarian rule, based on national identity and sovereignty claims, but with crucial transnational financial support. While these alternative visions often coexist within each Member State (reflecting the conflicting preferences of different social, political, and economic constituencies), increasingly they have become hallmarks of Member States, or blocs thereof, which are openly facing each other in the EU arena. These conflicting visions unsettle the EU, making its future uncertain.

As such, this chapter is structured as follows. Section 2 examines three old crises faced by the EU—the euro-crisis, the migration crisis, and the rule of law crisis—explaining how these have tested the unity of the EU27 in the field of Economic and Monetary Union (EMU), migration, and the respect for EU foundational values. Section 3 examines three new crises faced by the EU—the problem of enlargement, the fight against climate change, and the response to Covid-19—exposing in particular the divisions that have emerged among the EU27 in dealing with the catastrophic human and economic toll of the health pandemic. Section 4 explains how the crises shattering the EU have brought to light three competing visions of integration and conceptualizes the alternative ideas of polity, market, and autocracy at play. Section 5, finally, reflects on what this means for the prospects of integration besides Brexit and concludes.

2. Old Crises

Brexit was by no means the only crisis the EU had to deal with. In fact, well before the UK decided to leave the EU, the EU27 had been weathering a number of other crises—in particular the euro-crisis, the migration crisis, and the rule of law crisis. Moreover, each of these continued to sour the whole period of the Brexit negotiations, leaving a lasting legacy of tensions among the EU27.

2.1 Euro-crisis

The euro-crisis represented a major stress test for Europe's EMU—with protracted economic and political consequences. The EU and its Member States responded to the financial instability of 2009–2012 by introducing a battery of legal and institutional reforms:[2] strengthening the fiscal rules of the Stability and Growth Pact (SGP); establishing a new European Stability Mechanism (ESM) to support Member States financially;[3] and centralizing bank supervision and resolution. Moreover, the European Central Bank (ECB) took decisive steps to save the Eurozone.[4] However, responses to the euro-crisis were driven by a narrative that blamed the crisis on irresponsible public spending—and this approach caused a host of economic and political problems. On the one hand, the measures adopted to respond to the euro-crisis left a trail of divergence in the macro-economic performances of the Member States, with low growth and high unemployment in some countries:[5] a fact visible in Greece, where the end of the third bail-out programme in 2018 was accompanied by commitments to maintain 'a primary surplus of 2.2% of GDP on average in the period from 2023 to 2060'[6]—a target which most observers

---

[2] See further Federico Fabbrini, *Economic Governance in Europe* (OUP 2016).
[3] See Treaty Establishing the European Stability Mechanism, 2 February 2012 http://www. european-council.europa.eu/media/582311/05-tesm2.en12.pdf.
[4] See ECB President Mario Draghi, speech at the Global Investment Conference, London, 26 July 2012 (stating that the ECB will 'do whatever it takes to save the euro').
[5] See Kerstin Bernoth et al, 'Happy Birthday? The euro at 20', study commissioned by the European Parliament Economic Affairs Committee, January 2019.
[6] Eurogroup statement on Greece, 22 June 2018.

regarded as impossible to meet.[7] On the other hand, the management of the euro-crisis fuelled nationalist movements in a number of Member States, which openly started calling to leave the Eurozone: a fact visible in Italy, following the 2018 parliamentary elections.[8]

At the same time, the euro-crisis tainted inter-state relations, complicating efforts to deepen EMU[9]—which remains incomplete.[10] In fact, despite a series of high-level reports from the EU institutions and their leaders calling for completing EMU,[11] the EU27 have been unable to overcome national divisions. On the contrary, regional groups of EU Member States have increasingly faced each other with alternative plans for the future of EMU. In particular, while Southern states—Italy, France, Spain, Portugal, Greece, Malta, and Cyprus: caucusing together as the Med7—vocally pushed for the establishment of a central fiscal capacity with stabilization function, as well for a European deposit insurance scheme (EDIS),[12] a group of Northern states—led by the Netherlands, and including also Denmark, Sweden, Finland, Ireland, Estonia, Latvia, and Lithuania,[13] as well as on occasions Czechia and Slovakia,[14] in a coalition known as the a new Hanseatic League—resisted any step towards more burden sharing, calling rather for greater ESM surveillance of national budgets.

In this context, progress in deepening the EMU to prepare the Eurozone for the next crisis has been limited.[15] In particular, even though

---

[7] See Jeromin Zettelmeyer et al, 'How to Solve the Greek Debt Problem' Peterson Institute for International Economics Policy Brief 10/2018.

[8] See Roberto D'Alimonte, 'How the Populists Won in Italy' (2019) 30 *Journal of Democracy* 114.

[9] See also French President Emmanuel Macron, speech, Athens, 7 September 2017 (defining the eurocrisis as 'une forme de guerre civile interne').

[10] See ECB President Mario Draghi, speech at the session of the plenary of the European Parliament to mark the 20th anniversary of the euro in Strasbourg, 15 January 2019 (stating that 'EMU remains incomplete').

[11] See Four Presidents' Final Report, 'Towards a Genuine EMU', 5 December 2012; Five Presidents' Report, 'Completing Europe's EMU', 22 June 2015; and European Commission reflection paper on 'The Deepening of Economic and Monetary Union', 31 May 2017.

[12] See Declaration of the summit of the Southern European Union countries, Madrid, 10 April 2017.

[13] Shared views of the Finance Ministers from Denmark, Estonia, Finland, Ireland, Latvia, Lithuania, the Netherlands and Sweden, 6 March 2018.

[14] Shared views of the Finance Ministers from the Czech Republic, Denmark, Estonia, Finland, Ireland, Latvia, Lithuania, the Netherlands, Sweden and Slovakia on the ESM reform, 1 November 2018.

[15] See Henrik Enderlein et al, 'Repair and Prepare: Growth and the Euro after Brexit', Bertelsmann Stiftung & Jacques Delors Institut 2016.

in November 2018 France managed on paper to convince Germany to support a Eurozone budget with counter-cyclical functions to stabilize EMU against economic shocks,[16] this initiative was stalled in the Euro Summit.[17] In the end, after much debate, the Eurogroup in an inclusive format (also open to non-Eurozone Member States) reached in June 2019 a minimalist consensus on a package deal of reforms, which included an enhancement of the ESM and the creation of a budgetary instrument for competitiveness and convergence (BICC).[18] However, the purpose of BICC explicitly excluded a stabilization function, effectively still leaving the Eurozone without a fiscal capacity.[19] Moreover, despite repeated calls, the Eurogroup made no progress on the establishment of EDIS, the third pillar of the EU banking union, which is regarded as essential in avoiding a doom loop between banks and sovereign defaults in the Eurozone[20]— suggesting that the ideological divide between risk reduction and risk sharing remains a stumbling block towards completing EMU.[21]

2.2 Migration Crisis

The migration crisis was another dramatic challenge for the integrity of the EU, which put the functioning of both the Schengen free-movement zone and the European Common Asylum System (ECAS) under severe strain and had lasting consequences on inter-state relations among the EU27.[22] Faced in the summer of 2015 with the sudden arrival of over a million people fleeing war in the Middle East and global poverty, the EU and its Member States struggled to develop a coordinated response. While

---

[16] See Franco-German Proposal on the architecture of a Eurozone Budget within the Framework of the European Union, 16 November 2018.

[17] See Euro Summit statement, 14 December 2018, PRESS 790/18.

[18] Council of the EU, Term sheet on the Budgetary Instrument for Convergence and Competitiveness, 14 June 2019.

[19] Federico Fabbrini, 'A Fiscal Capacity for the Eurozone', study commissioned by the European Parliament Constitutional Affairs Committee, February 2019.

[20] See also European Commission Communication, 'Deepening Europe's Economic and Monetary Union: Taking stock four years after the Five Presidents' Report', 12 June 2019, COM(2019) 279 final, 10 (stating that 'regrettably, the impasse that characterized the past several years has persisted and no tangible progress has been made' on EDIS).

[21] See also Federico Fabbrini & Marco Ventoruzzo (eds), *Research Handbook on EU Economic Law* (Edward Elgar Publishing 2019).

[22] See generally Cathryn Costello, *The Human Rights of Migrants and Refugees in European Law* (OUP 2015).

the EU attempted to outsource to third countries (with dubious human rights records) the task of controlling the EU's external borders, notably by striking a deal with Turkey,[23] a major rift on how to manage migration emerged between the Western EU Member States, which called for burden sharing and humanity in the treatment of asylum seekers, and Eastern Member States, which staunchly resisted any form of solidarity and refused asylum on ethnic homogeneity grounds to migrants coming from mostly Muslim countries. In fact, relations between Member States soured to the point that Luxembourg Interior Minister Jean Asselborn even suggested that Hungary should be expelled from the EU for the way it treats migrants.[24]

In particular, while the cornerstone of the ECAS, the Dublin regulation,[25] required Member States with external borders to process asylum applications of third country nationals entering the EU Schengen zone, Italy and Greece were overwhelmed by this unprecedented influx of migrants. Responding to this emergency situation, the Council of the EU in September 2015 adopted by majority a temporary relocation mechanism to the benefit of Greece and Italy, which foresaw the proportional relocation of 160,000 asylum seekers to the other EU Member States.[26] However, although this number was ludicrous given the total number of migrants entering the EU, Poland, Hungary, Czechia, and Slovakia—a group known as Visegrad—vehemently opposed this course of action. Hungary and Slovakia challenged the Council decision in the European Court of Justice (ECJ). And although in September 2017 the ECJ confirmed its full legality,[27] Hungary, Poland, and Czechia bluntly refused to comply with it. As a result, even though the ECJ later confirmed that refusal to participate in the relocation mechanism was a breach of EU

---

[23] See EU–Turkey statement, 18 March 2016, press release 144/16.

[24] Madeline Chambers & Marton Dunai, 'EU should expel Hungary for mistreating migrants, Luxembourg minister says', *Reuters*, 13 September 2016.

[25] See Regulation (EU) No 604/2013 of the European Parliament and of the Council of 26 June 2013 establishing the criteria and mechanisms for determining the Member State responsible for examining an application for international protection lodged in one of the Member States by a third-country national or a stateless person, OJ 2013 L 180/31.

[26] See Council Decision (EU) 2015/1523 of 14 September 2015 establishing provisional measures in the area of international protection for the benefit of Italy and of Greece, OJ 2015 L239/146; and Council Decision (EU) 2015/1601 of 22 September 2015 establishing provisional measures in the area of international protection for the benefit of Italy and Greece, OJ 2015 L 248/80.

[27] See Cases C-643/15 and C-647/15 *Slovakia & Hungary v Council of the EU*, ECLI:EU:C:2017:631.

law,[28] no concrete support was offered by the Eastern Member States to the worst-hit coastline EU countries.[29]

In fact, the question of how to deal with the ongoing arrival of asylum seekers to the external borders of EU Member States has continued to divide the EU27. Even though in 2015 the Commission put forward a proposal to overhaul ECAS, including a permanent relocation mechanism,[30] the plan has failed to make any real progress in the European Council.[31] As a result, France launched a coalition of the willing to break the deadlock at EU level, convening 13 EU Member States to set up a solidarity-based system to manage the disembarkation and relocation of asylum seekers on a voluntary basis.[32] However, the legacy of the crisis combined with the inequities of the system fuelled xenophobic political movements across Europe, which called in the North for the suspension of Schengen[33] and in the South for the outright pushback of migrants.[34] In the end, while the European Court of Human Rights (ECtHR) ruled that forced return of migrants violated the prohibition of non-refoulement,[35] and the ECJ ruled that Hungarian legislation on the detention of migrants was in breach of EU human rights law,[36] the management of migration remained an unresolved issue—as evident also in February 2020, when Turkey temporarily opened its border with Greece and a new wave of migrants attempted to enter the EU, only to be faced with a violent pushback.[37]

---

[28] See Joined Cases C-715/17, C-718/17, and C-719/17 *Commission v Poland, Hungary & the Czech Republic*, ECLI:EU:C:2020:257.

[29] See European Commission, 'Thirteenth report on relocation and resettlement', 13 June 2017, COM(2017) 330 final (describing the implementation of the relocation scheme as utterly 'insufficient').

[30] See European Commission Communication, 'A European Agenda on Migration', 13 May 2015, COM(2015) 240 final.

[31] See European Council Conclusions 28 June 2018, EUCO 9/18, para. 12.

[32] French government, Réunion informelle sur le migrations en Méditerranée: Conclusions de la Présidence, 22 July 2019.

[33] See European Commission Communication, 'Preserving and strengthening Schengen', 27 September 2017, COM(2017) 570 final.

[34] See Andrew Geddes & Andrea Pettrachin, 'Italian migration policy and politics: Exacerbating paradoxes' (2020) 12 *Contemporary Italian Politics* 227.

[35] See ECtHR, *Hirsi Jamaa v Italy*, App. No. 27765/09, judgment of 23 February 2012.

[36] See Joined Cases C-294/19 PPU and C-925/19 PPU *FMS and Others*, ECLI:EU:C:2020:294; and Case C-808/18 *Commission v Hungary*, ECLI:EU:C:2020:493.

[37] See also Council of Europe Commissioner for Human Rights Dunja Mijatović, Letter to European Commissioners Margaritis Schinas and Ylva Johansson, 9 March 2020 (emphasizing that the EU should respect the prohibition of non-refoulement).

2.3   Rule of Law Crisis

An even more dramatic crisis that the EU has faced is the rule of law crisis. Although the EU protects fundamental rights,[38] and Article 2 TEU proclaims that the EU 'is founded on the values of respect for human dignity, freedom, democracy, equality, [and] the rule of law', since the early 2010s a number of Member States have experienced legal and political developments that have openly challenged basic constitutional principles such as the independence of the judiciary, separation of powers, and the fairness of the electoral process.[39] This backsliding is particularly acute among those Member States who joined the EU in the 2004/2007 enlargements, and is part of a broader right-wing, populist political trend at play in former Communist countries—including also in Eastern Germany. Threats to the rule of law constitute a major danger for the EU.[40] Yet Hungarian Prime Minister Viktor Orbán proudly defended this path, explicitly arguing that his country was intent on establishing an authoritarian democracy.[41] The Hungarian example has increasingly served as a template for other new EU Member States, notably Poland and Romania. But rule of law issues have emerged also in Slovakia and Malta.[42]

Although arguably with excessive delay, the EU institutions have started to take action against this phenomenon. In particular, as mentioned in Chapter 3, in preparation for the next multi-annual EU budget, the European Commission proposed to introduce a mechanism to freeze structural funds for EU Member States who failed to respect the rule of law.[43] In addition, in December 2017 the Commission activated the Article 7 TEU procedure against Poland, calling on the Council to determine that the country faced a clear risk of a serious breach of the rule of

---

[38] See further Federico Fabbrini, *Fundamental Rights in Europe* (OUP 2014).

[39] See Laurent Pech & Kim Lane Scheppele, 'Illiberalism Within: Rule of Law Backsliding in the EU' (2017) 19 *Cambridge Yearbook of European Legal Studies* 3.

[40] See European Commission Communication, 'A New EU Framework to Strengthen the Rule of Law', 11 March 2014, COM(2014) 158 final.

[41] Hungarian Prime Minister Viktor Orbán, speech at the XXV. Bálványos Free Summer University and Youth Camp, 26 July 2014 (stating that 'the new state that we are building is an illiberal state, a non-liberal state').

[42] See European Parliament resolution of 28 March 2019 on the situation of the rule of law and the fight against corruption in the EU, specifically in Malta and Slovakia, P8_TA(2019)0328.

[43] European Commission proposal for a regulation of the European Parliament and the Council on the protection of the Union's budget in case of generalised deficiencies as regards the rule of law in the Member States, 2 May 2018, COM(2018) 324 final.

law.[44] And in September 2018 the European Parliament (EP) approved a resolution to initiate the same process against Hungary.[45] Nevertheless, despite support from several Member States,[46] limited progress has been made by the Council in deciding whether corrective action against Hungary and Poland was necessary.[47] In fact, in the first semester of 2019, when the rotating presidency of the Council was held by Romania—a Member State which had been strongly criticized by the EP for its rule of law record and limited efforts to fight corruption[48]—the discussion of the Article 7 TEU procedure against Poland and Hungary was even removed from the agenda of the General Affairs Council.[49]

In this context, a major role has been taken by the ECJ. Ruling in preliminary reference proceedings from Ireland,[50] the ECJ held that rule of law backsliding—if this resulted in the reduction of the due process rights of a convicted person, to be assessed cases by case—could justify a court decision not to execute a European Arrest Warrant toward Poland.[51] Moreover, ruling in infringement proceedings brought by the Commission, the ECJ stopped Poland from giving effect to a highly controversial law which altered the composition of the state Supreme Court in breach of EU principles on the independence and impartiality of the judiciary,[52] and also struck down Polish legislation instituting disciplinary

---

[44] European Commission reasoned proposal in accordance with Article 7(1) Treaty on European Union for a Council Decision on the determination of a clear risk of a serious breach by the Republic of Poland of the rule of law, 20 December 2017, COM(2017) 835 final.

[45] European Parliament resolution of 12 September 2018 on a proposal calling on the Council to determine, pursuant to Article 7(1) of the Treaty on European Union, the existence of a clear risk of a serious breach by Hungary of the values on which the Union is founded, P8_TA(2018)0340.

[46] See French Assemblée Nationale résolution relative au respect de l'état de droit au sein de l'Union européenne, 27 November 2018, n° 194; Benelux Prime Ministers' Summit Joint Declaration, Luxembourg, 2 April 2019.

[47] See also European Parliament resolution of 16 January 2020 on ongoing hearings under Article 7(1) TEU regarding Poland and Hungary, P9_TA(2020)0014.

[48] European Parliament resolution of 13 November 2018 on the rule of law in Romania, P8_TA(2018)0446.

[49] See General Affairs Council, Outcome of meeting, 8 January 2019, Doc. 5039/19.

[50] See *Minister for Justice and Equality v Celmer* [2018] IEHC 119.

[51] See Case C-216/18 PPU *LM*, ECLI:EU:C:2018:586. The judgment of the ECJ is starting to be applied by national courts. See e.g. in Italy: Corte di Cassazione, Sesta Sezione Penale, n° 15294, judgment of 21 May 2020 (blocking the execution of a European arrest warrant from Italy to Poland and remanding the case to a lower court).

[52] See Case C-619/18 R *Commission v Poland*, Order of the Vice-President of the Court, 19 October 2018, ECLI:EU:C:2018:910; and Judgment of the Court, 24 June 2019, ECLI:EU:C:2019:531.

proceedings against judges.[53] Finally, the ECJ also invalidated Hungarian laws infringing the independence of academia,[54] and the freedom of non-governmental organizations.[55] Yet, while the ECJ has so far managed to command respect, its ability to halt the erosion of the rule of law based system at the national level is likely to face challenges in the medium term, given the absence of EU coercive power[56] and the unwillingness by the other EU Member States to mobilize against threats to the rule of law in forms analogous to what was done at the time of the Haider affair.[57] In fact, the rule of law and democratic backsliding seems to be worsening, rather than receding, across many new EU Member States.

3. New Crises

Since Brexit, the EU has been facing a new wave of crises. In particular, while significant divisions recently emerged among the EU27 on how to deal with enlargement and the fight against climate change, the explosion of the Covid-19 pandemic in March 2020—just weeks after the UK withdrawal—exposed the continuing difficulty faced by the EU in crisis governance.

3.1 Enlargement

A first taste of the continuing tensions among the EU27 post-Brexit emerged prominently in October 2019: at the same European Council meeting which approved the Withdrawal Agreement renegotiated between the European Commission and the UK government led by Boris Johnson,[58] the EU27 split on the controversial issue of enlargement.[59] In

---

[53] See Case C-791/19 R *Commission v Poland*, Order of the Court, 8 April 2020, ECLI:EU:C:2020:277.

[54] See Case C-66/18 *Commission v Hungary*, Opinion of Advocate General Kokott, delivered on 5 March 2020, ECLI:EU:C:2020:172.

[55] See Case C-78/18 *Commission v Hungary*, ECLI:EU:C:2020:476.

[56] See Andras Jakab & Dimity Kochenov (eds), *The Enforcement of EU Law and Values* (OUP 2017).

[57] Wojciech Sadurski, 'Adding Bite to Bark: The Story of Article 7, E.U. Enlargement, and Jörg Haider' (2010) 16 *Columbia Journal of European Law* 385.

[58] European Council Conclusions, 17 October 2019, EUCO XT 20018/19.

[59] European Council Conclusions, 18 October 2019, EUCO 23/19, para. 5.

particular, a major row erupted among Member States on whether to authorize accession talks with Albania and North Macedonia. While during the 2014–2019 European Commission term, then President Jean-Claude Juncker had clarified that no new Member State would join the EU under his watch,[60] the accession process had been subsequently relaunched—particularly in the context of the Prespa Agreement of 12 June 2018. This treaty, concluded between Greece and the then Former Yugoslav Republic of North Macedonia resolved a 30-year-old dispute on the name of North Macedonia—and the prospect of accession to the EU (and NATO) had been put forward as an incentive to conclude the deal.

However, the EU27 were heavily divided on the course to take, with especially France—with the backing of Denmark and the Netherlands—objecting to any bureaucratic automaticity in the accession process, and calling for greater political steering on decisions about enlargement.[61] In the absence of the necessary unanimity within the European Council, the issue was referred back to the European Commission, which on 5 February 2020 put forward a new methodology for accession negotiations. This confirmed a credible EU perspective for the Western Balkans, but also subjected the enlargement talks to further conditionality, with negotiations on the fundamentals, including the rule of law, to be opened first and closed last, and with the possibility of suspending the accession talks tout court.[62] On this basis, in March 2020, the Council of the EU gave the green light to the start of the enlargement, stabilization, and association process with North Macedonia and, with greater caveats, Albania.[63] However, it remains to be seen how far this will proceed,[64] as also evident from the fact that the Zagreb Declaration concluded by the leaders of the EU27 and the Western Balkan countries on 6 May 2020 did not mention the word 'enlargement'.[65]

---

[60] European Commission President-elect Jean-Claude Juncker, 'A New Start for Europe: My Agenda for Jobs, Growth, Fairness and Democratic Change. Political Guidelines for the next European Commission', 15 July 2014, 12.

[61] See French Non-Paper, 'Reforming the European Union accession process', November 2019.

[62] European Commission Communication, 'Enhancing the accession process: A credible EU perspective for the Western Balkans', 5 February 2020, COM(2020) 57 final, 2–3.

[63] Council of the EU, 25 March 2020, Doc. 7002/20.

[64] See Andi Mustafaj, 'Plaidoyer pour une vraie réforme du processus d'élargissement de l'Union européenne', Fondation Robert Schuman, April 2020.

[65] See Zagreb Declaration, 6 May 2020.

3.2 Climate Change

Another field in which tensions between the EU27 emerged prominently while the UK was about to exit the EU is that of the fight against climate change. Given growing scientific concerns for rising global temperatures and increasing awareness among the population for the consequences of climate change, national and international institutions have step by step endeavoured to develop a concerted action. In particular, at the international level the 2015 Paris Agreement adopted within the United Nations Framework Convention on Climate Change set global objectives to reach climate neutrality by 2050, which were accepted by a vast majority of states worldwide (including the United States, although it later withdrew from the agreement). At the EU level, however, the Commission proposed the 2030 climate and energy framework, with targets and measures for carbon emissions reduction, renewable energy consumption, and energy efficiency.[66] The new Commission, however, also endeavoured to take even more ambitious and binding initiatives.[67] After making the fight against climate change as one of the priorities of her mandate,[68] Commission President Ursula von der Leyen launched on 11 December 2019 a European Green Deal, which set a target of reducing EU greenhouse gas emissions to 50% by 2030, while also establishing a Just Transition Fund to facilitate Member States in the carbon transition.[69]

However, the proposals of the Commission exposed profound differences among the EU27, with in particular less economically developed Eastern Member States opposing the plan, which instead was mostly embraced by richer Western and Northern Member States, notably France.[70]

---

[66] See European Commission Communication, 'A policy framework for climate and energy in the period from 2020 to 2030', 22 January 2014, COM(2014) 015 final.

[67] See also Alessandro Monti & Beatriz Martinez Romera, 'Fifty shades of binding: Appraising the enforcement toolkit for the EU's 2030 renewable energy targets' (2020) 29 *Review of European Comparative and International Environmental Law* 1.

[68] European Commission President-candidate Ursula von der Leyen, 'A Union that strives for more: My agenda for Europe. Political Guidelines for the Next European Commission 2019-2024', 16 July 2019.

[69] See European Commission Communication, 'The European Green Deal', 11 December 2019, COM(2019) 640 final.

[70] See 'Eastern European countries threaten to wreck EU "Green Deal"', *Euronews*, 12 December 2020. The Polish government had long resisted complying also with an ECJ judgment blocking on environmental grounds the wood logging in the Białowieża Forest. See Case C-441/17 *Commission v Poland*, ECLI:EU:C:2018:255.

Hence, on 12 December 2019—in the same meeting in which heads of state and government welcomed the clarity coming from the UK general elections which delivered a stunning victory for Prime Minister Johnson and opened the door for the conclusion of the Brexit withdrawal process[71]—the European Council endorsed in principles the goals of the Paris Agreement but had to acknowledge that '[o]ne member state, at this stage, cannot commit to implement th[e] objective' of reaching climate neutrality by 2050—owing to the staunch opposition by Poland.[72] In fact, while to appease the hold-outs the EU27 welcomed the Commission proposal for a Just Transition Fund,[73] which was formalized in January 2020,[74] progress on the overall green package has been limited—also for the emergence of another, more dramatic, crisis.

3.3 Covid-19

The EU27 were just adjusting to the UK's withdrawal from the EU when 'a human tragedy of potentially biblical proportions'[75] fell upon them: the Covid-19 pandemic. As the virus started spreading rapidly across Europe, and indeed the world, EU Member States' governments rushed in March 2020 to take unprecedented public policy measures. In particular with death tolls spiking to shocking numbers, across the continent authorities imposed warlike lockdowns, closing schools, factories, and public facilities, banning the movement of persons, prohibiting public gatherings, and requisitioning properties essential to address the health crisis.[76] The immediate action by the EU Member States revealed a remarkable lack of coordination, with some countries unilaterally suspending the intra-EU export of medical devices, or introducing intra-EU border checks, also on goods—in blatant disregard of EU law.[77] In fact, Hungary even

---

[71] European Council Conclusions, 13 December 2019, EUCO XT 20027/19.

[72] See European Council Conclusions, 12 December 2019, EUCO 29/19, para. 1.

[73] Ibid para. 4.

[74] See European Commission proposal for a Regulation of the European Parliament and the Council establishing the Just Transition Fund, 14 January 2020, COM(2020) 22 final.

[75] See former ECB President Mario Draghi, 'We face a war against coronavirus and must mobilize accordingly', Op-Ed, *Financial Times*, 26 March 2020.

[76] See also joint document by the European Commission and the European Council, Joint European Roadmap towards lifting Covid-19 containment measures, 15 April 2020.

[77] See also European Parliament resolution of 17 April 2020 on EU coordinated action to combat the Covid-19 pandemic and its consequences, P9_TA(2020)0054.

abused Covid-19 to adopt emergency legislation which allowed the government to rule indefinitely by decree—effectively codifying into law authoritarian governance.[78]

Eventually, a more European response to Covid-19 started to take place—especially in tackling the socio-economic consequences of the pandemic. In particular, after some hesitation, the EU supranational institutions mobilized to support Member States worst hit by the health crisis. The European Investment Bank (EIB) developed a special Covid-19 investment scheme of €40 billion to support SMEs,[79] which was then complemented by a larger €200 billion programme backed by new Member States' guarantees.[80] The ECB launched a new pandemic emergency purchase programme, committing to buy public bonds and commercial paper in the financial markets up to €750 billion,[81] which was subsequently almost doubled in size to €1350 billion.[82] Moreover, important initiatives were taken by the Commission: this suspended the application of state aid rules;[83] called on the Council to trigger the SGP general escape clause putting on temporary hold fiscal rules;[84] activated the EU Solidarity Fund;[85] put forward a coronavirus response investment initiative to mobilize €37 billion of available cash reserves in the EU Structural and Investment Funds;[86] and also proposed the establishment of a

---

[78] See Act XII of 30 March 2020 on protecting against coronavirus (Hu.). Subsequently, on 16 June, the Hungarian Parliament voted unanimously to suspend the state of emergency. However it also passed a new law, which entered into force on the following day, on temporary sanitary measures that carried over many of the provisions of the old law. See Act LVIII of 17 June 2020 on transitional provisions of the termination of state of danger and on epidemic preparation (Hu.).

[79] See EIB press release, 'EIB group will rapidly mobilize up to €40 billion to fight crisis caused by Covid-19', 16 March 2020.

[80] See EIB press release, 'EIB Board approves €25 Billion Pan-European Guarantee Fund in response to Covid-19 crisis', 26 May 2020.

[81] See Decision (EU) 2020/440 of the European Central Bank of 24 March 2020 on a temporary pandemic emergency purchase programme (ECB/2020/17), OJ 2020 L 91/1.

[82] See ECB press release, 'Monetary policy decisions', 4 June 2020.

[83] See European Commission Communication, 'Temporary Framework for State aid measures to support the economy in the current Covid-19 outbreak', 20 March 2020, 2020/C 91 I/01.

[84] See Council of the EU, statement, 23 March 2020 (agreeing with the assessment of the Commission that the conditions to suspend the SPG were fulfilled).

[85] See Regulation (EU) 2020/461 of the European Parliament and of the Council of 30 March 2020 amending Council Regulation (EC) No 2012/2002 in order to provide financial assistance to Member States and to countries negotiating their accession to the Union that are seriously affected by a major public health emergency, OJ 2020 L 99/9.

[86] See Regulation (EU) 2020/460 of the European Parliament and of the Council of 30 March 2020 amending Regulations (EU) No 1301/2013, (EU) No 1303/2013 and (EU) No 508/2014 as regards specific measures to mobilise investments in the healthcare systems of Member States and in other sectors of their economies in response to the COVID-19 outbreak (Coronavirus Response Investment Initiative), OJ 2020 L 99/5.

European instrument for temporary support to mitigate unemployment risks in an emergency (SURE)—a reinsurance system designed to support the heavily pressurized national unemployment insurance regimes through loans backed up by Member States' guarantees.[87]

However, joint action by the EU intergovernmental institutions was much less forthcoming.[88] In fact, the EU27 split heavily on what new measures to put in place to sustain the economy during the pandemic and relaunch it afterwards. In particular, on 25 March 2020 a group of nine Eurozone states—France, Italy, Spain, Portugal, Greece, Slovenia, Belgium, Luxembourg, and Ireland—requested in a letter to the European Council President that the EU start 'working on a common debt instrument issued by a European institution to raise funds on the market on the same basis and to the benefit of all Member States'.[89] Yet, this proposal was fiercely rejected as an unacceptable effort of debt mutualization by Germany and the Netherlands, who instead called for using the ESM as a crisis response tool.[90] In this context, the European Council, meeting by video-conference for the third time in two weeks, failed to reach a deal[91]—and hence kicked the can down the road to the Eurogroup. Yet, the Eurogroup, meeting in an inclusive format (open to non-Eurozone Member States), did not have an easier time either: after three days of negotiation, on 9 April 2020 it came up with a half-baked compromise, which envisioned tackling Covid-19 with both the ESM and a new Recovery Fund.[92] However, details on the latter were scant at best, confirming disagreement among the Member States on how to get the EU out of the Covid-19 crisis.[93]

On 18 May 2020, France and Germany jointly put forward an initiative for a European Recovery Fund—a temporary and targeted facility

---

[87] See Council Regulation (EU) 2020/672 of 19 May 2020 on the establishment of a European instrument for temporary support to mitigate unemployment risks in an emergency (SURE) following the Covid-19 outbreak, OJ 2020 L 159/1.

[88] See also Italian President Sergio Mattarella, statement, 27 March 2020.

[89] See Joint Letter by Belgium, France, Greece, Ireland, Italy, Luxembourg, Portugal, Slovenia, and Spain to European Council President Charles Michel, 25 March 2020.

[90] See Dutch Finance Minister Wopke Hoekstra, statement at the Twedde Kammer, 7 April 2019 https://debatgemist.tweedekamer.nl/debatten/eurogroep.

[91] See Joint statement of the Members of the European Council, 26 March 2020.

[92] See Council of the EU, Report on the comprehensive economic policy responses to the Covid-19 pandemic, 9 April 2020.

[93] See also Sebastian Grund et al, 'Sharing the Fiscal Burden of the Crisis', Hertie School Jacques Delors Centre Policy Paper, 7 April 2020.

connected to the new EU budget and worth €500 billion, to be funded by borrowing on the markets, and to be disbursed through grants (rather than loans) to the Member States worst hit by the crisis.[94] Nevertheless, on 20 May 2020, a coalition of Nordic countries—the Netherlands, Austria, Denmark, and Sweden—responded to the Franco-German initiative with a joint non-paper which instead proposed the creation of an Emergency Fund disbursing loans to Member States, de facto along the model of the ESM.[95]

In the end, on 27 May 2020 the Commission presented an ambitious proposal for an EU recovery plan, with a revamped multi-annual financial framework (MFF) for 2021–2027,[96] and particularly a new €750 billion recovery instrument ('Next Generation EU'), to be disbursed two-thirds in grants and one-third in loans, and to be financed through the emission of common debt.[97] Nevertheless, the Commission proposal was met with criticism from the Visegrad countries—Poland, Hungary, Czechia, and Slovakia—which complained that the instrument introduced a rule of law conditionality and did not set aside sufficient funding for lower income Member States.[98] Given these divisions, on 19 June 2020 the European Council failed to muster the unanimity needed,[99] prompting the organization, a few days afterwards, of a new summit.[100]

Eventually, after five days of meeting on 17, 18, 19, 20, and 21 July 2020—in the longest European Council since the Nice summit of 2001— heads of state and government of the EU27 managed to find a deal on the EU recovery plan, and relatedly on the next MFF.[101] Yet, to muster the necessary unanimity, the Commission plan for 'Next Generation EU' was amended, reducing the overall size of grants from €500 billion to €390 billion, and increasing the loans component from €250 billion

---

[94] See French–German Initiative for the European Recovery from the Coronavirus Crisis, 18 May 2020.

[95] See Austria, Denmark, the Netherlands, and Sweden, Non-paper EU support for efficient and sustainable Covid-19 recovery, 20 May 2020.

[96] See European Commission Communication, 'The EU budget powering the recovery plan for Europe', 27 May 2020, COM(2020) 442 final.

[97] See European Commission Communication, 'Europe's moment: Repair and Prepare for the Next Generation', 27 May 2020, COM(2020) 456 final.

[98] See Government of the Czech Republic press release, 'V4 common lines regarding the Multiannual Financial Framework/Next Generation EU', 11 June 2020.

[99] See European Council President Charles Michel, remarks, 19 June 2020, 415/20.

[100] See also European Council President Charles Michel, statement, 10 July 2020.

[101] See European Council Conclusions, 21 July 2020, EUCO 10/20.

to €360 billion.[102] Moreover, to appease the recalcitrant Nordic Member States, the European Council agreed to cap the size of the next MFF,[103] and maintain their rebates;[104] and to obtain the crucial support of Central and Eastern Member States, it watered down the obligation to respect the rule of law as a condition to receive EU funding.[105] These choices, coupled with unsettled agreement on the governance arrangements of 'Next Generation EU',[106] and its future funding,[107] however, were met with some scepticism by the EP, which under the treaty has a veto right on the approval of the MFF.[108] As such, further negotiations seem to lie ahead,[109] suggesting that the elaboration of a consensual post-Covid-19 EU recovery strategy remains a work in progress—as will be further discussed in Chapter 5.

4. Competing Visions

The crises that the EU27 weathered in recent years have exposed deep fissures in the fabric of the union. The euro-crisis caused a cleavage between Northern and Southern states: the migration crisis between Western and Eastern states; the rule of law crisis, and partially enlargement, between new and old Member States; the climate change crisis between rich and poor states; while Covid-19 exposed a diagonal divide between states in the South and West of Europe—which are, interestingly, mostly Catholic—and states in the North and East of Europe—which are mostly Protestant. While the preferences of each Member State in all these crises sometimes differ—and therefore national stances did not map neatly one crisis onto another—it is possible to identify a number of recurrent positions that the EU27 have articulated across these separate crisis-related

---

[102] Ibid para. A6.
[103] Ibid para. A23.
[104] Ibid para. A30.
[105] Ibid para. A24.
[106] Ibid para. A19.
[107] Ibid para. 145.
[108] See European Parliament resolution of 23 July 2020 on the conclusions of the extraordinary European Council meeting of 17-21 July 2020, P9_TA(2020)0206.
[109] See also Irish Minister of Finance Paschal Donohoe, Letter of candidature for the role of Eurogroup President, 25 June 2020 (indicating the importance of 'building bridges' between Member States).

debates. These positions effectively reflect alternative visions of what European integration is, and ought to be.

Therefore, it is worth attempting to conceptualize these competing visions, with the aim of explaining their consequences on the future of the EU. For analytical purposes, I suggest in particular that three visions are currently competing: a first that sees the EU as a polity project; a second that instead sees the EU as mostly a market project; and a third that sees the EU as an autocracy-enhancing tool. Two caveats are obviously in order here. First, in some cases these visions are explicitly articulated, but often they are undertheorized, and thus have to be uncovered from the words and deeds of key political actors. As such, these conceptual frames are scholarly constructs, designed to reveal, and make sense of, a complex reality. Secondly, while some EU Member States' governments have become the embodiment of these alternative visions, all of these visions really coexist and compete within each Member State—with different social, political, and economic constituencies embracing alternative preferences and promoting them. As such, the categorization advanced here inevitably operates an oversimplification of reality, and should not be interpreted rigidly as permanently boxing states. Yet, distinguishing between these three alternative visions of Europe is crucial to understand the EU27's direction of travel, and the challenges ahead.

4.1   Polity

Increasingly detectable in the struggles to address Europe's multiple crises is a vision of integration which aspires towards greater commonality of action—on the understanding that EU Member States and their people somehow represent a community of destiny.[110] I call this a 'polity vision' of Europe. A recurrent feature of this vision of integration is the call for greater solidarity—including burden sharing in dealing with the costs of the euro-crisis, with the sudden influx of migrants, as well as with the unprecedented consequences of the Covid-19 pandemic. Moreover, this vision of integration pursues an ambitious EU budget, which must be adequate to achieve a manifold set of common objectives. At the same

---

[110] See ceteris paribus Ernest Renan, *Qu'est-ce qu'une nation?* [1882].

time, this vision believes in the idea that the EU must rest on a number of foundational values such as respect for the rule of law, democracy, and human rights—while being sceptical of further enlargements, until the EU has deepened.

Arguably, the epitome of this vision of integration is offered today by France, under the leadership of its President Emmanuel Macron. Since taking office in 2017, President Macron has consistently spoken in favour of a sovereign, united, and democratic Europe[111]—ambitiously calling for a relaunch of the EU after Brexit.[112] In policy terms, President Macron has forcefully positioned France in favour of devising common, innovative solutions at EU level to tackle the euro-crisis,[113] the migration crisis,[114] and Covid-19.[115] Moreover, the French government pushed for ambitious goals in fighting climate change[116]—and, as mentioned in Chapter 3, it favoured an increase of the EU budget, so as to make it rise to the height of expectations. At the same time, France has taken a firm position against backsliding in the rule of law,[117] while also pulling the break on the enlargement process until mechanisms of reversibility and rule of law conditionality were introduced.[118] As President Macron put it before the EP elections in an open letter addressed to all European citizens (and written in the 22 official languages of the EU) *pour une renaissance européenne*, 'Europe is not just a market. It is a project [... of] European civilisation that unites, frees and protects us.'[119] And as he repeated in an interview given in the early stages of the responses to Covid-19: 'We are at a moment of truth, which is to decide whether the European Union is a political project or just a market project. I think it is a political project.'[120]

---

[111] See French President Emmanuel Macron, speech at Université La Sorbonne, 26 September 2017.

[112] French President Emmanuel Macron, speech at the award of the Prix Charlemagne, Aachen, 11 May 2018.

[113] See n 16.

[114] See n 32.

[115] See n 89.

[116] See n 70.

[117] See n 46.

[118] See n 61.

[119] French President Emmanuel Macron, Letter, 4 March 2019 https://www.elysee.fr/es/emmanuel-macron/2019/03/04/pour-une-renaissance-europeenne.fr.

[120] French President Emmanuel Macron, Interview, *Financial Times*, 17 April 2020.

4.2 Market

The position that President Macron appeared to criticize, however, also has the features of a fully fledged vision of integration—one based on the idea that EU Member States are together as commercial partners trading with each other to maximize their national wealth.[121] I call this a 'market vision' of Europe. A recurrent feature of this vision of integration is the plea for more individual responsibility—with objections to risk sharing in the field of EMU, and to increases in the EU budget, even in the responses to Covid-19, which may result in further inter-state transfers. At the same time, this vision of integration is cold towards common action in the management of migration, which is a responsibility of Member States with external borders. Yet, this vision of integration is committed to the respect of rules—not only fiscal ones—and as such is vocal against breaches of the rule of law, and democratic backsliding; and despite supporting the prospects of an enlarged EU internal market to new countries, is also cautious against the accession of new Member States until they have proven their ability to fulfil the preset regulatory criteria.

While perhaps the UK government may have historically best represented this vision of integration, today its face seems to have become the government of the Netherlands—although its leader never really systematized this stance. In fact, Dutch Prime Minister Mark Rutte openly dismissed as senseless the idea of articulating a grand vision of Europe, calling instead for a much more down-to-earth approach—but one based on the view of the EU 'as the ultimate example of the power of international cooperation and free trade'.[122] In fact, the Dutch government steadfastly resisted efforts to deepen EMU[123] and develop common debt instruments to address the Covid-19 pandemic.[124] Moreover, as pointed out in Chapter 3, the Netherlands opposed the expansion of the EU budget—cobbling together coalitions of like-minded Nordic states to defend these positions. However, the Dutch government supported EU

---

[121] See ceteris paribus Adam Smith, *The Wealth of Nations* [1776].
[122] Dutch Prime Minister Mark Rutte, speech at the European Parliament, Strasbourg, 13 June 2018 (later dismissing in the debate the ideas of grand plans by saying that if you have a vision you need to consult a doctor).
[123] See n 13.
[124] See n 90.

coordinated responses to the challenge of climate change,[125] and has been uncompromising in demanding respect for the rule of law,[126] which it regarded as essential also for the functioning of the EU internal market, including by pre-accession countries.[127] As Prime Minister Rutte put it to the EP in June 2018, 'a deal is a deal'—and the EU must rest on rules to prosper in an unruly world.[128]

4.3 Autocracy

The not-so-subtle target of Prime Minister Rutte's speech was obviously a third vision of integration, one explicitly intent on restoring sovereignty, reneging democracy, and restricting the rule of law—but with EU money. I call this an 'autocracy vision' of Europe. A recurrent feature of this vision of integration is the appeal to national identity[129]—with objections towards any form of solidarity in the relocation of migrants who are seen as a threat to the ethnic homogeneity of the people. Moreover, this vision of integration openly defies the foundational values of the EU—including respect for the separation of powers, the independence of the judiciary, and the freedom of the press or civil society—but gladly supports the further Eastward enlargement of the EU, particularly if it allows for the accession of likeminded nation states. At the same time, this vision welcomes redistributive policies in the fiscal sector—and therefore fully supports an ambitious EU budget in the new MFF negotiations, with the resulting financial transfers. In fact, for sponsors of this vision of Europe, the EU is an essential element of the transformation of the state into an autocracy, as it provides the resources to maintain national growth and economic well-being through a system of crony capitalism and corruption.

Clearly, the paradigmatic example of this vision of integration is Hungary under the rule of Prime Minister Viktor Orbán—who has largely been taken as a role model also by the governing party in Poland.

---

[125] See n 70.
[126] See Dutch Prime Minister Mark Rutte, speech at the Bertelsmann Stiftung, Berlin, 2 March 2018.
[127] See n 61.
[128] Rutte (n 122).
[129] See Federico Fabbrini & Andras Sajó, 'The Dangers of Constitutional Identity' (2019) 25 *European Law Journal* 457.

As underlined in Chapter 3, Prime Minister Orbán clearly positioned Hungary among the friends of cohesion in the negotiations on the new EU budget—and called for greater solidarity and financial transfers in favour of Eastern states, both in the context of the responses to Covid-19[130] and as extra payback for supporting the green deal.[131] But his government unrepentantly resisted any solidarity whatsoever when this entailed the relocation of asylum seekers adopted to tackle the migration crisis—even flouting the ECJ's orders to this end.[132] And he openly spoke in favour of transforming Hungary into an illiberal democracy[133]—a plan he faithfully put into action by packing courts, changing the electoral laws, and silencing civil societies in his direct favour. In fact, by exploiting the Covid-19 pandemic to push through Parliament emergency legislation enabling the government to rule by decree,[134] Prime Minister Orbán walked the final steps to turn Hungary into a fully fledged autocracy.

5. Conclusion

This chapter has examined the EU besides Brexit. In addition to managing the UK's withdrawal, the EU27 had recently to face a plurality of other crises. However, in dealing with these old and new challenges, the EU27 struggled to develop a coordinated response and solve once and for all these pressing problems. In fact, the stream of seemingly uninterrupted crises afflicting the EU in the last decade—from the euro-crisis to the migration crisis and the rule of law crisis—climaxing in the dramatic Covid-19 pandemic, profoundly divided the EU27, leaving deep scars in the fabric of the union. In all of these crises contexts, as well as in the debates on enlargement and the fight against climate change, the EU crises governance system proved unable to overcome cleavages among Member States, which increasingly started caucusing in regional blocs facing each other and unleashing centrifugal pulls in the architecture of the EU.

---

[130] See n 98.
[131] See n 70.
[132] See n 28.
[133] Orbán (n 41).
[134] See n 78.

In fact, as the chapter has emphasized, the profound divisions among the EU27 reflect the rise of competing visions of the project of European integration[135]—what I called a polity, a market, and an autocracy conception of Europe's finality. These conceptual categories are not rigid—and usually these alternative visions coexist and compete within each Member State. Yet, these different *Weltanschauungen* have increasingly come to be embodied by EU countries or groups thereof—and have become harder to reconcile, weighing ominously on the future of the EU27. In fact, although the capacity of the EU to muddle through must not be underestimated, in recent years differentiation has increasingly emerged as the mechanism allowing the EU to advance in the face of opposition, as reluctantly acknowledged also by the EP.[136] While differentiated integration is surely not new in the EU, in recent times this dynamic has reached a new height—as evident in the establishment of even the new European Public Prosecutor's Office (EPPO), a crucial new authority designed to fight financial crime through enhanced cooperation between only 20 of the EU Member States,[137] given the staunch resistance by the others, which include countries with significant issues of rule of law backsliding.[138]

However, differentiated integration has limits. On the one hand, there are questions about its level of inclusivity. For example, as pointed out in Chapter 2 in the analysis of the Permanent Structured Cooperation in the field of defence (PESCO), 25 Member States joined the project of military cooperation, but their different strategic priorities ultimately prompted the establishment of a separate European Intervention Initiative, for a smaller group. On the other hand, differentiation may lead to decoupling, with the possible emergence of smaller unions within the EU.[139] In fact, recent efforts at deepening Franco-German cooperation, which resulted even in the establishment of a Franco-German Parliamentary Assembly

---

[135] See also Hungarian Prime Minister Viktor Orbán, Interview, *La Stampa*, 1 May 2019 (stating that 'oggi ci sono già tre Europe, ma fingiamo sia soltanto una [today there are already three Europes, but we pretend it is only one]') (my translation).

[136] European Parliament resolution of 17 January 2019 on differentiated integration, P8_TA-PROV(2019)0044.

[137] See Council Regulation (EU) 2017/1939 of 12 October 2017 implementing enhanced cooperation on the establishment of the European Public Prosecutor's Office, OJ 2017 L 283/1.

[138] See also ECtHR, *Kövesi v Romania*, App. No. 3594/19, judgment of 5 May 2020.

[139] See Sergio Fabbrini, *Europe's Future: Decoupling and Reforming* (CUP 2019).

charged to 'formuler des propositions sur toute question intéressant les relations franco-allemandes en vue de tendre vers une convergence des droits français et allemande',[140] point in that direction. In conclusion, it is clear that pragmatic solutions are no panacea beyond the short term, and the structural weaknesses of the EU system of governance exposed by crises must be tackled with proper constitutional reforms.

---

[140] Accord parlamentaire franco-allemand, 25 March 2019, Art. 6.

5

The EU after Brexit

Constitutional Reforms

1. Introduction

The European Union (EU) stood united vis-à-vis the United Kingdom (UK) during Brexit. However, the EU27 heavily divided in responding to the multiple other crises that have shattered the EU in the past decade besides Brexit. The difficulties of the EU in successfully weathering old and new crises, which are grounded in conflicting visions of integration, pose a major challenge to the future of Europe after Brexit. While surely the EU is not new to facing crises,[1] the recent series of prolonged and unsolved crises left deep scars in the fabric of the union. Yet, because the fate of (con)federal associations depends also on their ability to counterbalance centrifugal pressures,[2] it is essential for the EU to avoid any complacency and to embark, after the UK withdrawal, on the reform process it started debating after the UK referendum. The purpose of this chapter is to examine the EU after Brexit, making the case in favour of constitutional reforms, and mapping the obstacles and opportunities to achieve this objective.

As the chapter argues, the case for reforming the EU is strong. To begin with, the EU system of governance suffers from a number of shortcomings—which have been patently exposed in the course of the recent crises. From a substantive viewpoint, the EU still lacks critical competences, and it only has limited enforcement powers and resources

---

[1] See e.g. Piers Ludlow, 'Challenging French Leadership in Europe: Germany, Italy, the Netherlands and the Outbreak of the Empty Chair Crisis of 1965-1966' (1999) 8 *Contemporary European History* 231.
[2] See Hans Vollaard, *European Disintegration: A Search for Explanations* (Palgrave 2018).

Brexit and the Future of the European Union. Federico Fabbrini, Oxford University Press (2020). © Federico Fabbrini. DOI: 10.1093/oso/9780198871262.003.0005

to carry out its functions. From an institutional viewpoint, then, recent crises have exasperated the intergovernmental trend in the EU, but this mode of decision-making has seeded discord among the EU27 and has always delivered too little, too late in crisis time and beyond. Moreover, the case for reforming the EU is made even stronger by the exigencies of the post-Covid-19 recovery. While the outline of the EU recovery plan is still subject to negotiations, the European Commission initiative to roll out an unprecedented economic stimulus package calls for adequate constitutional adjustments to back this up structurally.

However, as the chapter points out, if the objective of strengthening the EU's effectiveness and legitimacy is of the highest order, there are obstacles to reforming the EU. In fact, the EU treaty amendment procedure—by conditioning revisions to the EU treaties on the approval by all the Member States meeting in an intergovernmental conference (IGC) and unanimous ratification at the national level—represents a formidable hurdle. However, in recent years—particularly in responding to the euro-crisis—EU Member States have increasingly resorted to inter se international agreements concluded outside the EU legal order—which have done away with the unanimity requirement. In the context of Europe's Economic and Monetary Union (EMU), therefore, Member States have been able to overcome the problem of the veto by using separate international treaties—and this practice opens up new opportunities to push for a reform agenda also outside the EMU.

As such, the chapter is structured as follows. Section 2 outlines the main objectives of an EU reform agenda, explaining on the one hand how the EU system of governance suffers from major substantive and institutional weaknesses that need to be addressed, and emphasizing on the other hand how the exigencies of the post-Covid-19 EU recovery will inevitably require constitutional adaptations. Section 3, then, analyses the obstacles to reform, focusing on the formal rules for treaty change enshrined in EU primary law, and underscoring how the requirement of unanimous ratification for treaty changes which is set therein creates a veto problem threatening any reform effort. Section 4 considers opportunities for reform, by pointing out how Member States have increasingly resorted to inter se international agreements outside the EU legal order to avoid ratification crises, and how this has overcome the problem of the veto. Section 5 concludes.

2. Objectives of Reform

Elsewhere I have argued that Brexit would compel the EU to reform its basic documents[3]—not least to remove the UK from the list of Member States to which 'the Treaties shall apply' pursuant to Article 52 Treaty on European Union (TEU). In fact, from a formal point of view, references to the UK are made in several provisions of EU primary law, including Article 355 Treaty on the Functioning of the European Union (TFEU), and these clauses could not be amended—and indeed were not amended—by the Withdrawal Agreement. Contrary to Article 49 TEU, which regulates enlargement and allows 'adjustments to the Treaties on which the Union is founded' to be made through the accession treaties, Article 50 TEU does not foresee anything analogous for withdrawal. As a result, a future treaty revision would appear to be necessary to clean the EU's constitutive treaties from references to the UK, which have now become moot.

Nevertheless, there are arguably much more fundamental reasons for reopening the working site of EU treaty change. On the one hand, the EU system of governance presents a number of shortcomings—which have been pitifully exposed by the EU's difficulties in dealing successfully with the crises described in Chapter 4. On the other hand, some recent developments—and most notably the EU's strategy for a post-Covid-19 recovery—create an additional urge to back up this substantive restructuring of the EU's powers and responsibilities with corresponding constitutional adjustments. Therefore, if strong challenges are likely to arise owing to the conflicting visions of Europe's future, an equally strong case can be made for renewing the EU and relaunching integration. After Brexit, and Covid-19, the effectiveness and legitimacy of the EU must be improved—and this requires appropriate constitutional reforms.

---

[3] See Federico Fabbrini, 'Brexit and EU Treaty Reform' in Federico Fabbrini (ed), *The Law & Politics of Brexit* (OUP 2017), 271.

2.1 The Shortcomings of the EU System of Governance

The old and new crises recently faced by the EU, described in Chapter 4, have revealed the limitations of the current EU system of governance. In fact, the difficulties of the EU in solving once and for all any of the pending crises are a consequence of the substantive and institutional weaknesses of the current EU constitutional architecture. From a substantive point of view, the competences of the EU are limited. Indeed, the principle of conferral enshrined in Article 5(2) TEU proclaims that 'the Union shall act only within the limits of the competences conferred upon it by the Member States in the Treaties'. At the same time, Article 2 TFEU categorized EU competences, distinguishing between those exclusive of the EU and those shared between the EU and the Member States, while also creating a blurred class of coordinating, supporting, and supplementing competences 'in certain areas and under certain conditions laid down in the Treaties', where the EU must 'carry out actions to support, coordinate or supplement the actions of the Member States without thereby superseding their competence in these areas'. However, for instance, a policy area where the EU only has supporting competence is health,[4] the relevance of which has been dramatically exposed by the Covid-19 pandemic.[5]

Moreover, even when the EU has formally conferred competences to intervene in a given sector, the instruments that are made available under the treaties to act are often inadequate for the challenges at stake. In fact, recent crises have highlighted a serious enforcement problem for EU law—with increasing instances of Member States' non-compliance with fully valid EU norms.[6] This is particularly the case in the context of migration,[7] as well as the rule of law:[8] neither infringement proceedings nor the threat of Article 7 TEU procedure have done much to redress the cavalier attitude of Visegrad states vis-à-vis Council decisions on the relocation of migrants, or ECJ rulings enjoining the implementation of domestic laws

---

[4] Art. 168, TFEU.
[5] See Chapter 4, section 3.3.
[6] See Carlos Closa & Dimitry Kochenov (eds), *Reinforcing Rule of Law Oversight in the European Union* (CUP 2018).
[7] See Chapter 4, section 2.2.
[8] See Chapter 4, section 2.3.

which have imperilled the independence of the judiciary. Yet cases of out-right defiance of EU law, often under colour of national constitutional identity claims,[9] have multiplied themselves in recent years, showing that the EU institutions have very little ability to compel obedience of EU law in recalcitrant Member States.[10] However, it has become evident that the absence of substantive enforcement tools to make sure that 'the law is ob-served'[11] uniformly and consistently across the EU poses a major threat to the project of European integration as a *Rechtsgemeinschaft*.[12]

From an institutional point of view, then, the EU suffers from major weaknesses.[13] In fact, recent crises have unearthed and accel-erated a major shift in the form of governance of the EU: the rise of intergovernmentalism.[14] Institutions such as the European Council[15] and the Eurogroup[16] have come to acquire a leading function in EU decision-making. As Uwe Puetter has argued, this is not a haphazard development; rather, it is the result of a deliberate choice made at the time of the Treaty of Maastricht to transfer new core state competences at the EU level without empowering the supranational institutions.[17] Be that as it may, in the last decade the European Council has become 'ever mightier'.[18] In fact, the European Council today meets much more frequently than what is foreseen in Article 15 TEU, and is regularly involved in deciding the agenda of the EU and its Member States across the board.[19] The European Council played a dominant role in EMU,[20] but has also emerged as crucial in other areas of policy-making—from migration[21] to enlargement,[22] the

---

[9] Federico Fabbrini & András Sajó, 'The dangers of constitutional identity' (2019) 25 *European Law Journal* 457.

[10] See Mark Dawson, 'Coping with Exit, Evasion, and Subversion in EU Law' (2020) 21 *German Law Journal* 51.

[11] Art. 19, TEU.

[12] See Julio Baquero Cruz, *What's Left of the Law of Integration?* (OUP 2018).

[13] See further Federico Fabbrini, 'The Institutional Origins of Europe's Constitutional Crises' in Tom Ginsburg et al (eds), *Constitutions in Times of Financial Crises* (CUP 2019), 204.

[14] See Sergio Fabbrini, *Which European Union?* (CUP 2015).

[15] Art. 15, TEU.

[16] Protocol 14.

[17] Uwe Puetter, *The European Council and the Council: New Intergovernmentalism and Institutional Change* (OUP 2014), 68.

[18] Editorial, 'An ever mighty European Council – Some recent institutional developments' (2009) 46 *Common Market Law Review* 1383.

[19] See Frederic Eggermont, *The Changing Role of the European Council in the Institutional Framework of the European Union* (Bruylant 2012).

[20] See Chapter 4, section 2.1.

[21] See Chapter 4, section 2.2.

[22] See Chapter 4, section 3.1.

fight against climate change,[23] and now of course health and the responses to the Covid-19 pandemic[24]—not to mention the negotiations on the next multi-annual financial framework (MFF).[25] In fact, the European Council has increasingly sidelined other EU institutions, including the Commission, the Council, and the European Parliament (EP).

However, the rise of the European Council as the power-house of the EU institutional structure has created important problems. Firstly, the European Council has deepened the pre-existing cleavages between Member States, fuelling the resurgence of a clash between conflicting national interests. In fact, this is an inevitable consequence of the structural composition of the European Council and the electoral incentives under-pinning it. Although a number of scholars have sought to mythologize the European Council as a bucolic institution in which Member States can reconcile their interests and find consensus through deliberation,[26] the reality is that the European Council is made up of national leaders—whose job it is to represent and promote the national interest.[27] But because EU Member States often have conflicting national interests—and opposite visions of the future of Europe, as explained in Chapter 4—it is unsurprising that disagreement has emerged in the European Council's functioning. With heads of state and governments going to Brussels with the aim of winning the best deal for their home countries, clashes between national leaders representing conflicting national interests have become a regular feature of European Council life, with negative feedback in the European public debate.[28]

Secondly, in an institution which structurally favours the clash between conflicting national interests, it has become inevitable for the leaders representing the larger and more powerful Member States to gain the upper hand. Although formally speaking all heads of state

---

[23] See Chapter 4, section 3.2.

[24] See Chapter 4, section 3.3.

[25] See Chapter 3, section 4.2.

[26] See Luuk van Middelaar, *The Passage to Europe: How a Continent Became a Union* (Yale University Press 2013).

[27] See Petya Alexandrova & Arco Timmermans, 'National interest versus the common good: The Presidency in European Council agenda setting' (2012) 52 *European Journal of Political Research* 316.

[28] See Ingolf Pernice et al, *A Democratic Solution to the Crisis: Reform Steps towards a Democratically Based Economic and Financial Constitution for Europe* (Nomos 2012), 83.

and government sitting at the European Council table are equal, in reality state power matters—and some Member States are more powerful than others.[29] As Jonas Tallberg has explained, bargaining within intergovernmental institutions is the result of several sources of power and 'differences between large and small Member States' shape inter-state relations within the European Council.[30] Aggregate states' sources of power play the most fundamental role in explaining negotiation in the European Council, with the result that larger Member States can dominate the decision-making process. In this context, it is not surprising that Germany has emerged as the dominant player in defining the EU agenda.[31] Yet, this has raised a major challenge to the anti-hegemonic nature of the EU project.[32] It is evident that a system of governance that structurally disfavours the interests of smaller/weaker members vis-à-vis larger/mightier ones deeply undermines the fabric of the EU and its promise of continental pacification.[33]

In conclusion, the increase of intergovernmentalism as the leading mode of EU governance has decreased the effectiveness and legitimacy of the EU, as proven by the systematic difficulties of the EU to tackle the crises of the last decade. The structural incentive for each member of the European Council is to focus on the interests of the state where he/she is elected—not the interest of the EU as a whole. Owing to its composition, the European Council has fuelled inter-state conflicts, rather than taming them. And while conflict is part of politics,[34] domination by larger/mightier states has become the formula to solve inter-state disagreement. Yet this institutional state of affairs has undermined the legitimacy of the measures decided by the

---

[29] See Mark Dawson & Floris de Witte, 'Constitutional Balance in the EU after the Euro-Crisis' (2013) 76 *Modern Law Review* 817.

[30] Jonas Tallberg, 'Bargaining Power in the European Council' (2008) 46 *Journal of Common Market Studies* 685.

[31] See William Paterson, 'The Reluctant Hegemon? Germany Moves Center Stage in the European Union' (2011) 49 *Journal of Common Market Studies* 57.

[32] See Federico Fabbrini, 'States' Equality v States' Power: the Euro-crisis, Inter-state Relations and the Paradox of Domination' (2015) 17 *Cambridge Yearbook of European Legal Studies* 1.

[33] See Simone Bunse & Kalypso Nicolaïdis, 'Large versus Small States: Anti-Hegemony and the Politics of Shared Leadership', in Erik Jones et al (eds), *The Oxford Handbook of the European Union* (OUP 2012), 249, 251.

[34] See Damian Chalmers, 'The European Redistributive State and a European Law of Struggle' (2012) 18 *European Law Journal* 667, 686.

European Council.[35] In the end, as Sergio Fabbrini has underlined, decision-making within the European Council has always delivered too little, too late, since heads of state and government have faced challenges in reaching agreement on the measures to be taken, and then met selective non-compliance by some Member States in the implementation of the agreed measures.[36]

2.2 The Exigencies of the EU Recovery

If addressing the EU's current substantive and institutional weaknesses is thus essential to enhance the EU's effectiveness and legitimacy, the need for reforming the EU is further compounded by the exigencies of the post-Covid-19 recovery. In fact, while the EU institutions and the Member States were initially slow in devising a coordinated response to the pandemic, as shown in Chapter 4, they have subsequently put forward ambitious plans—which will necessitate further adjustments to the EU constitutional architecture.[37] In particular, on 27 May 2020 the Commission put forward a proposal for a European recovery plan, which—in order to repair the economic damage created by the health crisis and to prepare the EU for the next generation—dramatically increased the EU resources, revamping the next MFF 2021–2027,[38] and creating to the side of this a new €750 billion recovery instrument ('Next Generation EU'), to be distributed to the Member States two-thirds in grants and one-third in loans.[39] Moreover, in a major break with the past, the Commission proposed to fund the recovery plan by the emission of new EU debt on the financial markets (rather than states' transfers), to be repaid after 2028 and before 2058 through an increase of the headroom

---

[35] See Vivien Schmidt, *Europe's Crisis of Legitimacy* (OUP 2020).

[36] See Sergio Fabbrini, 'Intergovernmentalism and Its Limits' (2013) 46 *Comparative Political Studies* 1003, 1022.

[37] See also joint document of the European Council and the European Commission, A Roadmap for Recovery: Towards a more resilient, sustainable and fair Europe, 21 April 2020.

[38] See European Commission Communication, 'The EU budget powering the recovery plan for Europe', 27 May 2020, COM(2020) 442 final.

[39] See European Commission Communication, 'Europe's moment: Repair and Prepare for the Next Generation', 27 May 2020, COM(2020) 456 final.

in the own resource ceilings,[40] and prospectively the introduction of new EU taxes.[41]

The Commission's grand plan—which builds on prior proposals by Spain,[42] and France and Germany jointly,[43] and tracks the strategy endorsed by the EP[44]— represents a major step forward in the federalization of the EU.[45] Indeed, as I had pointed out in a report commissioned by the EP Constitutional Affairs (AFCO) Committee, contrary to all other federal unions by aggregation, the EU lacks a fiscal capacity[46]—and this significantly limited its ability to act, as it emerged in the context of the euro-crisis,[47] and the early stages of the Covid-19 crisis.[48] Even though the spirit and the letter of the EU treaties require the EU budget to be funded by own resources, as explained in Chapter 3, the EU budget is for the most part today financed by contributions from the Member States.[49] As a result, EU countries consider the contributions they make to the EU budget as *their* money, and aggressively measure the difference between their contributions to, and their receipts from, the EU budget. This has created an embarrassing spectacle, visible at every new MFF negotiation, revealing the unsustainability of a system where Member States quarrel about what they pay into, and get from, the EU budget.[50]

From this viewpoint, therefore, the Commission's project for an EU Recovery Instrument,[51] and especially the Recovery and Resilience

---

[40] See Commission amended proposal for a Council Decision on the system of Own Resources of the European Union, 28 May 2020, COM(2020) 445 final.

[41] See also Leaders of the main EP Parliamentary Groups, Manfred Weber et al, Letter to the European Council, 18 June 2020 (indicating that the EP 'will give its consent to the next MFF only if a basket of new own resources is introduced').

[42] See Spain Non-paper on a European recovery strategy, 19 April 2020.

[43] See French-German Initiative for the European Recovery from the Coronavirus Crisis, 18 May 2020.

[44] See European Parliament resolution of 15 May 2020 on the new multiannual financial framework, own resources and the recovery plan, P9_TA(2020)0124.

[45] See European Commission President Ursula von der Leyen, speech at the European Parliament, 27 May 2020.

[46] See also Federico Fabbrini, 'A Fiscal Capacity for the Eurozone', study commissioned by the European Parliament Constitutional Affairs Committee, February 2019.

[47] See Chapter 4, section 2.1.

[48] See Chapter 4, section 3.3.

[49] See Chapter 3, section 4.1.

[50] See Miguel Maduro, 'A New Governance for the European Union and the Euro', study commissioned by the European Parliament Constitutional Affairs Committee, September 2012.

[51] See European Commission proposal for a Council Regulation establishing a European Union Recovery Instrument to support the recovery in the aftermath of the Covid-19 pandemic, 28 May 2020, COM(2020) 441 final.

Facility designed to support states,[52] despite being designed as a temporary, one-off solution, constitutes a profound restructuring of the EU's constitutional architecture by endowing the EU with new fiscal powers derived by genuine own resources. After all, this is why the Commission's plan faced such strong resistance. In fact, as explained in Chapter 4, the Commission's initiative was met with pushbacks both by a group of Nordic Member States—the Netherlands, Austria, Denmark, and Sweden—which criticized it for being based on grants (rather than loans);[53] and by the Visegrad countries—Poland, Hungary, Czechia, and Slovakia—which criticized it for introducing rule of law conditionality and for not being generous enough towards lower income Member States.[54] As a result, the European Council meeting of 19 June 2020 was unable to find an agreement on the recovery plan[55]—revealing the difficulties of striking a compromise between a polity, a market, and an autocracy vision of the future of Europe post-Covid-19.

Yet, eventually, after five days of meeting on 17, 18, 19, 20, and 21 July 2020—in the longest European Council since the Nice summit of 2001—heads of state and government of the EU27 managed to find a deal on the EU recovery plan, and relatedly on the next MFF.[56] As explained in Chapter 4, this agreement required many compromises. In particular, to appease Nordic Member States, the European Council reduced the overall size of the grants component of 'Next Generation EU' from €500 billion to €390 billion, increasing the loans component from €250 billion to €360 billion.[57] Moreover, to obtain the crucial support of Central and Eastern Member States, it watered down the obligation to respect the rule of law as a condition to receive EU funding.[58] At the same time, the European Council left somehow unsettled the governance of 'Next Generation EU'—entrusting the management to the Commission, but subject to control of the Economic and Financial Committee, and with

---

[52] See European Commission proposal for a Regulation of the European Parliament and the Council establishing a Recovery and Resilience Facility, 28 May 2020, COM(2020) 408 final.

[53] See Austria, Denmark, the Netherlands, and Sweden, Non-paper EU support for efficient and sustainable Covid-19 recovery, 20 May 2020.

[54] See Government of the Czech Republic press release, 'V4 common lines regarding the Multiannual Financial Framework/Next Generation EU', 11 June 2020.

[55] See European Council President Charles Michel, remarks, 19 June 2020, 415/20.

[56] See European Council Conclusions, 21 July 2020, EUCO 10/20.

[57] Ibid para. A6.

[58] Ibid para. A24.

a back-up role for the European Council[59]—a point which was met with scepticism by the EP, which under the treaty has a veto right on the approval of the MFF.[60]

Nevertheless, the conclusions of the European Council represented an historic step forward for the EU. On the one hand, the European Commission was authorized for the first time to borrow substantive amounts of funds, totalling €750 billion 'on behalf of the Union on the capital markets'.[61] On the other hand, the EU also agreed on a roadmap to repay this common debt through new, genuine EU taxes. While the European Council agreed to increase the EU spending ceiling during the next MFF,[62] it also committed itself to 'work towards reforming the own resources system and introduce new own resources'.[63] In particular, the European Council indicated that as a first step a new plastic tax will be introduced and applied as of January 2021;[64] it called on the Commission to put forward proposals for a carbon border adjustment tax and a digital tax;[65] and it indicated readiness to discuss a new EU financial transaction tax during the next MFF.[66]

From this point of view, therefore, there is no doubt that the EU's recovery plan will necessitate important consequential EU reforms. From a substantive point of view, the establishment of a recovery and resilience facility forces a rethink of the powers to tax and spend conferred on the EU. On the one hand, Article 310(1) TFEU requires that '[t]he revenue and expenditure shown in the [EU] budget shall be in balance'—thus constraining the EU's ability to issue debt, unless the expenditure ceiling is raised accordingly. But this situation is harder to sustain with an enlarged budget. On the other hand, Article 311 TFEU allows the EU to 'adopt provisions for the harmonisation of legislation concerning turnover taxes, excise duties and other forms of indirect taxation to the extent that such harmonisation is necessary to ensure the establishment and

---

[59] Ibid para. A19.
[60] See European Parliament resolution of 23 July 2020 on the conclusions of the extraordinary European Council meeting of 17-21 July 2020, P9_TA(2020)0206.
[61] European Council Conclusions (n 56) para. A3.
[62] Ibid para. A9.
[63] Ibid para. 145.
[64] Ibid para. 146.
[65] Ibid para. 147.
[66] Ibid para. 149.

the functioning of the internal market and to avoid distortion of competition'. However, the EU does not currently have the power of direct taxation. Yet, this state of affairs severely reduces the EU's effectiveness—raising the question of whether the time has arrived for the EU to enjoy a competence to introduce new direct taxes.

Moreover, from an institutional point of view, there is no doubt that the recovery plan would also require adequate reforms to increase the legitimacy and accountability of the EU decision-making system in financial matters. On the one hand, if the EU increases its powers in the fiscal domain, the exclusion of the EP—which is only consulted by the Council in its decisions on the adoption of harmonized taxes,[67] and on the EU's own resources[68]—can no longer be justified, given the principle of 'no taxation without representation'.[69] On the other hand, if the EU needs to raise an increasing amount of resources, it is clear that the unanimity requirements for Council votes under Articles 113 and 311 TFEU is no longer sustainable[70]—with the consequence that more expedited steps need to be taken towards a more democratic and effective system of decision-making in tax matters based on qualified majority voting.[71]

In conclusion, the growing economic solidarity resulting from the EU post-Covid-19 recovery plan also raises a democracy challenge,[72] which can only be addressed through a reformed EU constitutional settlement, in which new substantive taxing and spending powers at EU level are matched by new institutional mechanisms of democratic legitimacy and accountability at that same level of government. In fact, even if responses to Covid-19 eschew the intergovernmental path that was taken in response to prior crises, notably the euro-crisis, and are built around the *méthode communautaire*,[73] reforms are needed to back up the recovery

---

[67] Art. 113, TFEU.

[68] Art. 311, TFEU.

[69] See Giacinto Della Cananea, 'No Representation without Taxation: the European Union' in Lina Papadopoulou et al (eds), *Legitimacy Issues of the European Union in the Face of the Crisis* (Nomos 2017), 95.

[70] See Sylvain Plasschaert, 'Towards an Own Resource for the European Union? Why? How? And When?' (2004) 44 *European Taxation* 470.

[71] See also European Commission Communication, 'Towards a more efficient and democratic decision making in tax policy', 15 January 2019, COM(2019) 8 final.

[72] See also Richard Young, 'Democracy is the Missing Link in EU Coronavirus Recovery Plans', Carnegie Europe, 13 May 2020.

[73] See also European Commissioner for Economic Affairs Paolo Gentiloni, speech at the Conference 'Progettiamo il Rilancio', 13 June 2020.

plan with adequate constitutional adaptations. And all this requires treaty reforms. Therefore, if the shortcomings of the EU system of governance are powerful reasons to engage again with constitutional engineering, the case for EU reform is further compounded by the exigencies of the EU's recovery. This raises the question of defining the obstacles and opportunities to achieve this objective of the highest order.

3. Obstacles to Reform

Reforming the EU treaties to adjust them to the needs and challenges of new generations is in itself nothing new. Over the last 28 years, the EU treaties have been subject to a 'semi-permanent treaty revision process'[74]—with four major overhauls occurring in short sequence: the Treaty of Maastricht of 1992, the Treaty of Amsterdam of 1996, the Treaty of Nice of 2001, and the Treaty of Lisbon of 2007. Nevertheless, the rules on EU treaty amendment are particularly cumbersome—most notably by requiring unanimous approval and ratification by all the Member States. This has created serious obstacles to reform, by giving veto powers to national players, with negative effects for the whole process.

3.1 The Rules on EU Treaty Amendment

The rules on EU treaty reform are currently enshrined in Article 48 TEU. This provision presents a number of innovative features.[75] Yet, the fundamentals of the treaty revision procedure in EU law have remained unchanged since the early stages of the process of integration: treaty changes must be approved unanimously by the Member States formally congressing into an IGC, and in order to enter into force they must be

---

[74] Bruno De Witte, 'The Closest Thing to a Constitutional Conversation in Europe: The Semi-Permanent Treaty Revision Process' in Neil Walker et al (eds), *Convergence and Divergence in European Public Law* (Hart Publishing 2002), 39.

[75] See Steve Peers, 'The Future of EU Treaty Amendments' (2012) 31 *Yearbook of European Law* 17.

ratified by all of them in accordance with their domestic constitutional requirements.[76] As stated in Article 48(4) TEU:

> A conference of representatives of the governments of the Member States shall be convened by the President of the Council for the purpose of determining by common accord the amendments to be made to the Treaties. The amendments shall enter into force after being ratified by all the Member States in accordance with their respective constitutional requirements.

Formally, Article 48 TEU foresees two mechanisms to amend the EU treaties: an ordinary revision procedure, and a simplified one. In both cases, pursuant to Article 48(2) TEU 'the Government of any Member State, the European Parliament or the Commission may submit proposals for the amendment of the Treaties to the Council', which shall forward these to the European Council. In some cases, however, a less burdensome, simplified procedure can be used. In particular, pursuant to Article 48(6) TEU, a simplified revision procedure can be resorted to 'for revising all or part of the provisions of Part Three of the TFEU relating to the internal policies and action of the EU. In this case, the European Council—acting by unanimity after consulting the EP and the Commission—may adopt a decision amending all or part of the provisions of Part Three of the TFEU, which 'shall not enter into force until it is approved by the Member States in accordance with their respective constitutional requirements'. However, because Article 48(6) TEU explicitly affirms that the simplified revision procedure 'shall not increase the competences conferred on the Union in the Treaties', effectively this mechanism can only be used only in limited cases.[77]

As a result, the main mechanism to reform the EU treaties is the ordinary revision procedure, which has codified in EU primary law the so-called convention method, originally experimented in the process that

---

[76] See Art. 96, ECSC Treaty.

[77] But see European Council Decision No 2011/199/EU of 25 March 2011, amending Article 136 TFEU with regard to a stability mechanism for Member States whose currency is the euro, OJ 2011 L 91/1 (using the simplified revision procedure to amend Article 136 TFEU by adding a paragraph that recognizes 'the Member States whose currency is the euro may establish a stability mechanism ...').

led to the Treaty establishing a European Constitution.[78] According to Article 48(3) TEU,

> if the European Council, after consulting the European Parliament and the Commission, adopts by a simple majority a decision in favour of examining the proposed amendments, the President of the European Council shall convene a Convention composed of representatives of the national Parliaments, of the Heads of State or Government of the Member States, of the European Parliament and of the Commission.

The Convention shall examine the proposals for amendments and shall adopt by consensus a recommendation which is then submitted for ultimate consideration to, and approval by, the IGC of the Member States' governments. Pursuant to Article 48(3) TEU the European Council may decide by a simple majority 'not to convene a Convention should this not be justified by the extent of the proposed amendments'—but it must obtain EP consent to do so: hence, the EP can insist on calling a Convention to examine proposals for revisions to the EU treaties.[79]

Article 48 TEU therefore puts in place a highly regulated process for amending the EU treaties. Admittedly, other provisions permit changes to EU primary law. As already mentioned, Article 49 TEU, which regulates enlargement, allows 'adjustments to the Treaties on which the Union is founded, which such admission entails', to be made in the context of accession agreements.[80] Moreover, a number of treaty provisions set up ad hoc amendment rules, effectively creating specialized treaty amendment procedures: for example, the European Council can unanimously modify the composition of the Commission, which is set in Article 17(5) TEU, effectively changing the treaty.[81] Finally, the so-called passerelle clause of Article 48(7) TEU allows the European Council, acting unanimously and

---

[78] See Jean-Claude Piris, *The Lisbon Treaty: A Legal and Political Analysis* (CUP 2010), 104.

[79] But see European Parliament resolution of 6 May 2010 on the draft protocol amending Protocol No 36 on transitional provisions concerning the composition of the European Parliament for the rest of the 2009-2014 parliamentary term, P7_TA(2010)0148 (giving its consent under Article 48(3) TEU to proceed with an IGC without a convention).

[80] See e.g. Act concerning the conditions of accession of the Republic of Croatia and the adjustments to the Treaty on European Union and the Treaty on the Functioning of the European Union, OJ 2012 L 112/25.

[81] See European Council Decision of 22 May 2013 concerning the number of members of the European Commission 2013/272/EU, OJ 2013 L 165/98.

with the consent of the EP, to change the voting rules in the Council (from unanimity to qualified majority voting, or from a special to the ordinary legislative procedure), effectively empowering it to amend the treaties in specific cases.[82]

Yet, Article 48 TEU is indeed the main route through which the EU treaties can be modified. And while the Lisbon Treaty has created a simplified revision procedure—which gives the European Council a direct treaty-making role—it is the ordinary revision procedure which overall remains paramount. At the same time, while the Lisbon Treaty has now constitutionalized the convention method—which entrusts the preparation of treaty reforms to a mixed body where representatives of national parliaments and EU institutions sit alongside representatives of national governments—ultimately, Article 48 TEU has reaffirmed the original arrangement dating back to the early European integration's treaties and carried over as an almost natural state of affairs: it is the EU Member States' governments, meeting in the IGC, that have the power to adopt changes to the treaties by common accord—and these amendments enter into force when they are ratified by *all* Member States in accordance with their domestic constitutional requirements.

3.2 The Problem of the Veto

As is well known, however, the unanimity requirement for treaty change has become a major constraint in reforming the EU. If the need to obtain unanimous consent from all EU Member States as a condition to change the EU treaties could have been understandable in a union of six members, the requirement is nowadays an element of gridlock for a union of 27 (after Brexit). In fact, ratification crises have characterized recent processes of treaty amendment. Voters in France and the Netherland rejected the Treaty establishing the European Constitution in 2005,[83] and in Ireland they voted down the Treaty of Nice in 2001, as well as the Treaty of Lisbon in 2007—requiring the European Council to scramble to find a solution,

---

[82] See Giuliano Amato, 'Future Prospects for a European Constitution' in Giuliano Amato et al (eds), *Genesis and Destiny of the European Constitution* (Bruylant 2007), 1271.

[83] See Nick Barber et al (eds), *The Rise and Fall of the European Constitution* (Hart Publishing 2019).

with additional reassurances added to the treaties that allowed in both cases a second, successful, vote.[84] As Dermot Hodson and Imelda Maher have explained, national parliaments, courts, and the people through referenda have become ever more important actors in the process of national ratification of EU treaties, hence increasing the veto points against EU reforms.[85] In particular, a quantitative analysis shows that EU Member States' 'constitutional rules and norms underpinning the negotiation and consent stages [of EU treaty amendments] have shifted to provide a more prominent role to parliaments, the people and the courts'.[86]

In Germany, for example, the Constitutional Court, the Bundesverfassungsgericht (BVerfG), has reviewed both ex ante the legality of new EU treaties, and ex post the action of the EU institutions; and its jurisprudence has drawn over time a number of red lines on possible future steps in European integration. While the BVerfG has never prevented the ratification of any EU treaty so far, its case law has restricted the room for negotiation by the German government on EU affairs.[87] In its *Lissabon Urteil*, the BVerfG has identified a core set of competences which belong to the heart of state sovereignty and which cannot be transferred to the EU.[88] In reviewing the German law for the election of the EP, the BVerfG has reaffirmed its view that the EP is not a real parliamentary assembly, as it does not elect a government, thus striking down any national threshold (*Sperrklausel*) for parties to obtain representation in the EP.[89] And in its judgments relating to the legal measures adopted to respond to the euro-crisis, the BVerfG has been adamant in claiming that efforts to stabilize the EMU should not undermine the budgetary sovereignty of the German Parliament, or the right to democracy.[90]

In fact, in May 2020 the BVerfG took the unprecedented step of declaring the European Central Bank (ECB) public sector purchase

---

[84] See Gráinne de Búrca, 'If at First you Don't Succeed: Vote, Vote Again: Analyzing the "Second Referendum" Phenomenon in EU Treaty Change' (2010) 33 *Fordham International Law Journal* 1472.

[85] Dermot Hodson and Imelda Maher, *The Transformation of EU Treaty Making: The Rise of Parliaments, Referendums and Courts since 1950* (CUP 2018).

[86] Ibid 16.

[87] See Sabino Cassese, 'L'Unione europea e il guinzaglio tedesco' [2009] *Giornale di diritto amministrativo* 1003.

[88] See BVerfG 123, 267 (2009).

[89] See BverfG 2 BvE 2/13, judgment of 26 February 2014.

[90] See BverfG 2 BvR 1390/12 ff, judgment (preliminary measures) of 12 September 2012.

programme (PSPP) illegal, and simultaneously declared a judgment of the European Court of Justice (ECJ) inapplicable in Germany.[91] Whereas in 2014 the BVerfG had already raised concerns for the monetary policy of the ECB,[92] but eventually retracted its views,[93] abiding by a judgment of the ECJ which had upheld the legality of the outright monetary transaction (OMT) programme,[94] in its recent judgment the BVerfG crossed the Rubicon and for the first time ever declared EU action ultra vires. In an arrogant ruling, the BVerfG refused to follow the judgment of the ECJ in *Weiss*[95]—which had already declared the PSPP compatible with the EU treaties—and imposed a three-month timeframe on the ECB to better explain the proportionality of its programme. The ruling of the BVerfG drew a strong response from the EU institutions, with the Commission preparing infringement proceedings.[96] In fact, there is no doubt that the BVerfG ruling represents an illegal breach of the principle of the supremacy of EU law, which is designed to guarantee the equality of the Member States before the treaties.[97] However, the judgment also constituted a dramatic awakening to the damage that national constitutional courts—often under a distorted rhetoric of constitutional pluralism—can do to EU integration.[98] Although the position of the BVerfG is in many ways exceptional,[99] other national constitutional courts, particularly captured courts in rule of law backsliding countries in Central and Eastern Europe, have taken similar stands of open defiance vis-à-vis the EU.[100]

---

[91] See BVerfG, 2 BvR 859/15, 2 BvR 980/16, 2 BvR 2006/15, 2 BvR 1651/15, judgment of 5 May 2020.

[92] See BverfG 2 BvR 2728/13 ff, order of 7 February 2014.

[93] See BverfG 2 BvR 2728/13 ff, judgment of 21 June 2016.

[94] See Case C-62/14 *Gauweiler*, ECLI:EU:C:2015:400.

[95] See Case C-493/17 *Weiss*, ECLI:EU:C:2019:1046.

[96] See European Commission President Ursula von der Leyen, statement, 10 May 2020, 20/846.

[97] See Federico Fabbrini, 'After the OMT Case: The Supremacy of EU Law as the Guarantee of the Equality of the Member States' (2015) 16 *German Law Journal* 1003.

[98] See further also Federico Fabbrini & Daniel Kelemen, 'With one court decision, Germany may be plunging Europe into a constitutional crisis', Op-Ed, *The Washington Post*, 7 May 2020.

[99] See Monica Claes, 'The Validity and Primacy of EU Law and the "Cooperative Relationship" between National Constitutional Courts and the CJEU' in Federico Fabbrini (ed), *The European Court of Justice, the European Central Bank and the Supremacy of EU Law*. Special Issue (2016) 23 *Maastricht Journal of European & Comparative Law* 151.

[100] See e.g. Magyarország Alkotmánybírósága Decision 22/2016 (XII. 5) AB (Hungary's Constitutional Court declaring the Council of the EU decision adopted during the migration crisis and imposing relocation of asylum seekers to be in violation of the country's constitutional identity, intended as enshrining an ethnically homogenous nation).

At the same time, while any treaty change would need to pass muster before national courts in some EU Member States, other countries are facing different kinds of constitutional constraints on the path towards greater integration. In Ireland, for instance, under the *Crotty* doctrine of the Supreme Court every EU treaty that entails a transfer of power from the national to the European level must be approved through a constitutional referendum.[101] As mentioned above, however, Irish voters rejected the last two EU reform treaties. In 2001, Ireland voted down the Treaty of Nice; and in 2007 the Treaty of Lisbon. On both occasions, the European Council took stock of the decision of the Irish voters and at the request of the Irish government produced official declarations aimed at reassuring Ireland of the fact that, among others, the EU treaties would not undermine the principle of Irish military neutrality.[102] Based on these reassurances, the Nice and Lisbon Treaties were put to a second vote, and eventually approved in 2002 and 2008 respectively.

Even in countries where there is no constitutional requirement for a referendum on treaty changes, political expediency may make such a step inevitable.[103] As the examples of Denmark and the Netherland highlight, however, the popular mood may be strongly against any further step in European integration. Hence, in December 2015 the Danish citizens voted against the proposal endorsed by the nation's government to abandon Denmark's opt-out on several measures in the field of criminal justice and police cooperation,[104] limiting the possibility of cooperation between the law enforcement agencies of Denmark and the other EU Member States. And in a consultative referendum in April 2016 the Dutch citizens voted against the Ukraine Association Agreement,[105] complicating the possibility for the EU to strengthen its economic ties with Ukraine. If one considers also the maverick July 2015 Greek referendum where a majority of voters rejected the terms of the draft third memorandum of understanding between Greece and its EU creditors,[106]

---

[101] See *Crotty v An Taoiseach* [1987] IESC 4.
[102] See Presidency Conclusions, European Council, 11–12 December 2008, Doc. 17271/08.
[103] See also Fernando Mendez, Mario Mendez, & Vasiliki Triga, *Referendums and the European Union* (CUP 2014).
[104] See Danish Parliament, *Resultat af folkeafstemning: Nej* http://retsforbehold.eu.dk/da/nyheder/2015/resultat.
[105] See Dutch Election Council, *Uitslag referendum Associatieovereenkomst met Oekraïne*
[106] See Greek government, *Euroelections* http://ekloges.ypes.gr/current/e/public/#

a picture of increasing popular wariness against the EU seems to emerge. And this highlights the difficulties that lie in pursuing a treaty revision process where every Member State has a veto.

It is precisely due to the obstacles inherent in Article 48 TEU that a number of proposals have been put forward to amend the EU treaty amendment procedure. After all, the requirement to obtain unanimous approval by all Member States to reform a treaty is actually exceptional from a comparative viewpoint. Indeed, international organizations which are much less integrated than the EU allow their constituting treaties to be changed with a super-majority vote: for example, the United Nations allows its Charter to be amended by a vote of two-thirds of the members of the General Assembly, provided changes are ratified in accordance with their constitutional requirements by two-thirds of its members, including all the five permanent members of the Security Council.[107] In the run-up to the Treaty establishing a European Constitution, therefore, it was suggested to replace unanimity with a super-majority vote of five-sixths of the Member States as the rule for the entry into force of the reform treaty.[108] While the Convention did not itself consider this option,[109] the Commission in a preliminary draft Constitution of the European Union promoted by then President Romano Prodi—and known as the Penelope project—embraced it.[110] In particular, anticipating the problems that the unanimity rule would produce in the ratification process, the Commission proposed that the Treaty establishing the European Constitution should ultimately enter into force if 'by a given date, five-sixths of the Member States have ratified this agreement'[111] and that the 'Member States which have not ratified are deemed to have decided to leave the Union'.[112] The Commission acknowledged that this

---

[107] Art. 108, UN Charter.

[108] See European University Institute Robert Schuman Centre for European Studies, 'Reforming the Treaties' Amendment Procedures', report submitted to the European Commission, 31 July 2000.

[109] But see Valéry Giscard d'Estaing, Interview, *Financial Times*, 11 November 2002, 4 (suggesting the need to have the new treaty enter into force even without the consent of all the then 25 Member States).

[110] See European Commission, Feasibility Study: Contribution to a Preliminary Draft Constitution of the European Union, 4 December 2002 https://www.europarl.europa.eu/meetdocs/committees/afco/20021217/const051202_en.pdf.

[111] Ibid XII.

[112] Ibid.

represented 'a break with Article 48 TEU',[113] but it stated that this was 'consistent with international law'[114] because sufficient guarantees applied to the hold-outs.

Yet, the Commission's plan was criticized at the time from a strict legal point of view[115]—and it ultimately never made it into the final treaty text endorsed by the European Convention. Rather—precisely in light of the failure of the Treaty establishing a European Constitution—Article 48(5) TEU now foresees that '[i]f, two years after the signature of a treaty amending the Treaties, four fifths of the Member States have ratified it and one or more Member States have encountered difficulties in proceeding with ratification, the matter shall be referred to the European Council'. Yet, this effectively leaves the resolution of a future ratification crisis to the goodwill of the heads of state and government in the European Council. While it has been suggested that the complexity of consent to treaty amendments in the EU is necessary for reasons of legitimacy,[116] in reality the Article 48 TEU procedure is so dysfunctional that Member States have increasingly sought to circumvent it in their efforts to reform the EU.[117]

4. Opportunities for Reform

As a consequence of the difficulties of changing the EU treaties, Member States have in very recent years explored with ever greater frequency other options to reform the EU. To overcome the disagreement characterizing an ever more heterogeneous EU, and avoid the deadlock resulting from the unanimity rule, coalitions of Member States have increasingly concluded inter se agreements outside the EU legal order, but closely connected to the functioning of the EU—particularly in the context of the

---

[113] Ibid.
[114] Ibid.
[115] See Bruno De Witte, 'Entry into Force and Ratification', in Bruno De Witte (ed), *Ten Reflections on the Constitutional Treaty for Europe* (European University Institute Robert Schuman Centre for Advanced Studies 2003), 203, 212.
[116] See Dermot Hodson & Imelda Maher, 'The Necessary Complexity of Consent: Rules and Norms in EU Treaty Making' (2019) 21 *Cambridge Yearbook of European Legal Studies* 297.
[117] See also Carlos Closa, 'Looking Ahead: Pathways of Future Constitutional Evolution of the EU', study commissioned by the European Parliament Constitutional Affairs Committee, November 2014.

responses to the euro-crisis. These new agreements have all enshrined provisions for their entry into force that do away with the unanimity requirement and overcome national vetoes.

4.1 The Use of Intergovernmental Agreements in EMU

EU Member States retain the possibility of entering into international agreements outside the EU legal order. Indeed, as Bruno De Witte has pointed out, EU Member States remain subjects of international law and as such they are free to conclude international agreements between themselves—either all of them or just a group thereof.[118] Because of their EU membership, however, this freedom is subject to several constraints. To begin with, inter se agreements concluded between the Member States may not contain norms conflicting with EU law proper and cannot derogate from either primary or secondary law.[119] In fact, the ECJ has not hesitated to strike down bilateral agreements concluded between Member States as inconsistent with EU law.[120] Moreover, there are limits to how Member States can enlist the work of the EU institutions in agreements concluded outside the EU legal order.[121] In particular, as the ECJ ruled in *Pringle*, states are entitled, in areas which do not fall under the EU exclusive competence, to entrust tasks to the EU institutions, outside the framework of the EU, only provided that those tasks do not alter the essential character of the powers conferred on those institutions by the EU treaties.[122]

Yet, besides these limitations, EU Member States have leeway to resort to international agreements concluded outside the EU legal order; and in concluding such agreements they can craft new rules governing ratification and entry into force—overcoming the unanimity requirement

---

[118] Bruno De Witte, 'The European Union as an International Legal Experiment' in Gráinne de Búrca & Joseph H. H. Weiler (eds), *The Words of European Constitutionalism* (CUP 2011).

[119] See Bruno De Witte, 'The Law as Tool and Constraint of Differentiated Integration', EUI RSCAS Working Paper 47/2019, 11.

[120] See e.g. Case C-284/16 *Slowakische Republik v Achmea*, ECLI:EU:C:2018:158 (striking down a bilateral investment treaty between the Netherlands and Slovakia as incompatible with EU law).

[121] See Steve Peers, 'Towards a New Form of EU Law? The Use of EU Institutions Outside the EU Legal Framework' (2013) 9 *European Constitutional Law Review* 37.

[122] See Case C-370/12 *Pringle*, ECLI:EU:C:2012:756, para. 158.

set in Article 48 TEU. This is precisely what has happened in the context of the responses to the euro-crisis, where Europe's EMU was reformed with treaties concluded outside the EU legal order.[123] In 2012, 25 out of the then 27 EU Member States signed up to the Fiscal Compact, which strengthened the rules of the EMU, notably by requiring contracting parties to constitutionalize a balanced budget requirement.[124] In 2012, the then 17 Eurozone Member States also concluded the treaty establishing the European Stability Mechanism (ESM), which endowed the EMU with a stabilization fund to support states facing fiscal crises.[125] And in 2014, 26 Member States also concluded an intergovernmental agreement which—in the framework of the nascent Banking Union, with its Single Supervisory Mechanism (SSM) and Single Resolution Mechanism (SRM)—established a Single Resolution Fund (SRF) to support credit institutions facing a banking crisis and set rules on the transfer and mutualization of the national contributions to the SRF.[126]

4.2 Overcoming the Veto

The Fiscal Compact, the ESM treaty and the intergovernmental agreement on the SRF, falling outside the scope of Article 48 TEU, had special rules on their entry into force. In particular, Article 14(2) of the Fiscal Compact foresaw that: 'This Treaty shall enter into force on 1 January 2013, provided that twelve Contracting Parties whose currency is the euro have deposited their instrument of ratification.' Article 48 of the ESM Treaty provided that: 'This Treaty shall enter into force on the date when instruments of ratification, approval or acceptance have been deposited by signatories whose initial subscriptions represent no less than 90% of the total subscriptions.' And Article 11(2) of the SRF agreement stated that 'This Agreement shall enter into force ... when instruments

---

[123] See Federico Fabbrini, *Economic Governance in Europe* (OUP 2016).

[124] Treaty on Stability, Coordination and Governance in the Economic and Monetary Union, 2 March 2012 http://www.eurozone.europa.eu/media/304649/st00tscg26_en12.pdf.

[125] See Treaty Establishing the European Stability Mechanism, 2 February 2012 http://www.european-council.europa.eu/media/582311/05-tesm2.en12.pdf.

[126] See Agreement on the transfer and mutualisation of contributions to the Single Resolution Fund, 21 May 2014 http://register.consilium.europa.eu/doc/srv?l=EN&f=ST%208457%20 2014%20INIT.

of ratification, approval or acceptance have been deposited by signatories participating in the [SSM] and in the [SRM] that represent no less than 90% of the aggregate of the weighted votes of all Member States participating in the [SSM] and in the [SRM]', as determined according to Article 3 of Protocol No 36 on transitional provisions, which assigned (until 2014) to each Member State a number of weighted votes proportional to population for calculating majorities in the Council.

For the first time in the history of the EU, therefore, the Fiscal Compact, the ESM treaty, and the SRF agreement bypassed the unanimity requirement for treaty change. In fact—while Article 14(3) of the Fiscal Compact clearly indicated that the treaty shall apply as from the date of its entry into force only to those states 'which have ratified it'—by requiring ratification by just 12 Eurozone countries, it set approval by a *minority* of EU Member States as a condition for its entry into force. Moreover, the overcoming of the unanimity requirement was even more striking in the case of the ESM: because Eurozone Member States contribute to the paid-in capital stock of the ESM pro rata—with each contracting party contributing on the basis of a proportional capital key distribution set in Annex II of the ESM treaty—by subjecting entry into force of the treaty to the ratification, approval or acceptance of states representing 90% of the ESM capital, Article 48 of the ESM treaty essentially conditioned the operation of the ESM to the positive vote of just the largest Eurozone countries. Similarly, the SRF agreement—while clarifying in Article 12 that the treaty shall apply only 'amongst the Contracting Parties that have deposited their instruments of ratification, approval or acceptance'—set a super-majority requirement for approval, connecting the importance of each Member State's ratification to its weighted vote in the Council of the EU.

The new ratification rules introduced in the Fiscal Compact, the ESM Treaty, and the SRF agreement were all designed to prevent a hold-out Member State from blocking the treaty from applying among the others. In fact, the explicit opposition by the UK to treaty change was the main reason why EU Member States decided to conclude the Fiscal Compact outside the EU legal order[127]—while admittedly reasons of German

---

[127] See Michael Gordon, 'The United Kingdom and the Fiscal Compact' (2014) 10 *European Constitutional Law Review* 28.

domestic politics played a larger role in pushing states to using an inter-governmental agreement, rather than an act of secondary EU law, for the SRF.[128] Be that as it may, the new rules on the entry into force of these EMU-related treaties profoundly changed the ratification game, because they shifted the costs of non-ratification to the hold-out Member States. In fact, the process of ratification of the Fiscal Compact in Ireland—the only Member State where a referendum was required—proved as much, as voters reluctantly endorsed the treaty, simply not to be left out from this initiative.[129] As a result, none of these EMU-related treaties faced is-sues in the national ratification procedures and they all entered into force as scheduled with all the Member States, including the reluctant ones, ul-timately on board.

In sum, by going outside the legal order of the EU—provided they did not do anything in breach of EU law proper—Member States have been able to reform the EU, and specifically EMU. By resorting to inter se agreements, Member States have overcome the strictures of Article 48 TEU, finding a solution to reform the EU which is more consonant to a union with more than two dozen members. In particular, by introducing ad hoc rules on the entry into force of the Fiscal Compact, the ESM treaty, and the SRF agreement, Member States have overcome the veto that in-heres to the EU treaty amendment rule and thus ultimately guaranteed the speedy entry into force of these new inter se agreements. Needless to say, the specific ratification rules set by these treaties are question-able. In particular, the veto power given only to the largest and wealthiest Member States in the ESM treaty has raised eyebrows.[130] Moreover, it was a matter of concern that recital 5 in the preamble of the ESM treaty con-ditioned the granting of financial assistance by the ESM to the ratification of the Fiscal Compact—effectively putting countries in financial difficul-ties under duress to sign up to the Fiscal Compact as a quid pro quo to get ESM support. However, there is no doubt that the overcoming of the

---

[128] See Federico Fabbrini, 'On Banks, Courts and International Law. The Intergovernmental Agreement on the Single Resolution Fund in Context' (2014) 21 *Maastricht Journal of European & Comparative Law* 444.

[129] See Roderic O'Gorman, 'An Analysis of the Method and Efficacy of Ireland's Incorporation of the Fiscal Compact' in Federico Fabbrini et al (eds), *The Constitutionalization of European Budgetary Constraints* (Hart Publishing 2014), 273.

[130] See Carri Ginter and Raul Narits, 'The Perspective of a Small Member State to the Democratic Deficiency of the ESM' (2013) 38 *Review of Central & Eastern European Law* 54.

unanimity rule of ratification in these agreements is an important precedent, which opens new opportunities to reform the EU more broadly.

5. Conclusion

This chapter has analysed the EU beyond Brexit. A strong case can be made in favour of reforming the EU. Despite the EU's successes in managing the UK's withdrawal, the EU27 faced a plurality of crises, which tested the integrity of the EU. In fact, all of these crises are connected to structural weaknesses in the EU's constitutional system. From a substantive viewpoint, the EU still lacks critical powers and resources and has only limited ability to enforce its laws in disobedient Member States. From an institutional viewpoint, then, the EU is increasingly prey to intergovernmental modes of decision-making, which however have decreased the legitimacy and the effectiveness of its action. These shortcomings must be tackled through constitutional reforms. In fact, the need for institutional and substantive changes to the EU is increased by the exigencies of the EU's post-pandemic recovery strategy, which by restructuring fiscal and democratic powers and responsibilities calls for a corresponding resettlement of the EU's constitutional architecture.

However, the EU reform agenda must reckon with the obstacles of treaty change. In fact, the EU treaty amendment procedure—which in its deep features has essentially remained unchanged since the heyday of integration—requires unanimous approval and ratification of any treaty change by all Member States. The existence of a veto, however, has created major difficulties—as proven by the recurrent ratification crises in the latest attempts at treaty change. Yet, it is precisely to overcome the problem of the veto that Member States have increasingly resorted to alternative pathways to reform. In the context of the euro-crisis, in particular, Member States have used intergovernmental agreements to reform EMU—and in these separate treaties concluded outside the EU legal order they have introduced new rules on entry into force that do away with the unanimity requirement. This practice represents an important precedent, which leaders at the national and supranational level should take into account as the EU eventually embarks on a broader reform process.

6

The EU beyond Brexit

The Conference on the Future of Europe

1. Introduction

The case for reforming the European Union (EU) after Brexit is strong. In fact, the EU27 opened a reflection on Europe's future already during Brexit, showing awareness of the need to respond to the United Kingdom (UK) withdrawal with a proper plan of action. Today, beyond Brexit, the debate on the future of Europe is eventually about to move from rhetoric to reality with the launch of the Conference on the Future of Europe. This idea originally belongs to French President Emmanuel Macron, who on 4 March 2019—in an open letter addressed to all European citizens (written in the 22 official languages of the EU) *pour une renaissance européenne*—recommended to convene 'with the representatives of the European institutions and the Member States, a Conference for Europe in order to propose all the changes our political project needs, with an open mind, even to amending the treaties'.[1] Since then, the initiative has been endorsed by the EU institutions, which have worked to kick-start the Conference in 2020.[2] The purpose of this chapter is to examine the EU beyond Brexit, discussing the plans, precedents, and prospects of the Conference on the Future of Europe and suggesting guideposts for its success.

As the chapter argues, the Conference on the Future of Europe is a very welcome initiative, constituting potentially a ground-breaking enterprise to reform the EU and increase its effectiveness and legitimacy. In fact, even though Covid-19 has delayed the launch of the Conference

---

[1] French President Emmanuel Macron, Letter, 4 March 2019 https://www.elysee.fr/es/emmanuel-macron/2019/03/04/pour-une-renaissance-europeenne.fr.

[2] A Joint Declaration by the EU institutions will formally mark the start of the process.

Brexit and the Future of the European Union. Federico Fabbrini, Oxford University Press (2020). © Federico Fabbrini. DOI: 10.1093/oso/9780198871262.003.0006

it has made it all the more necessary, by showing dramatically the weaknesses of the EU, and the urgency of its reform. From this point of view, the Conference on the Future of Europe can be an innovative model to renew the EU—analogous to previous out-of-the-box initiatives such as the Conference of Messina and the Convention on the Future of Europe which were crucial, at prior junctures of Europe's history, to restructure the EU and relaunch integration. However, in light of the obstacles to treaty reform, if the Conference on the Future of Europe is to succeed in its ambitious objective to reform the EU, it must tackle the key issue of the EU treaty change rules.

Therefore, the chapter puts forward possible avenues for further political integration in Europe. In particular—drawing from the practice of using intergovernmental agreements in the context of Europe's Economic and Monetary Union (EMU), examined in Chapter 5—it suggests that policy-makers involved in the Conference on the Future of Europe should resolve to draft a new treaty—call it a Political Compact—and submit it to a new ratification rule, which replaces the unanimity requirement with a super-majority vote. Channelling the outcome of the Conference process in a separate legal document, with new entry-into-force-rules will be a pre-condition for the success of the initiative—regardless of the substantive content of the compact, which would be for the Conference itself to deliberate on. Clearly, this prospect raises new questions, and the success of the endeavour cannot be taken for granted. However, the EU faces the challenges of a defining moment, hence the destiny of the Conference will shape the EU's future.

As such the chapter is structured as follows. Section 2 overviews the plans for the institutional organization and constitutional mandate on the Conference on the Future of Europe put forward by the EU institutions and the Member States, both pre-Covid-19 and post-Covid-19. Section 3 maps the precedents of the Conference on the Future of Europe—notably the historical examples of the Conference of Messina and the Convention on the Future of Europe—and highlights some of the conditions for their successes and failures. Section 4 discusses the prospects of the Conference on the Future of Europe and suggests that, to make this initiative a reform success, policy-makers involved in this process should consider producing a Political Compact, whose entry into force would be subject to less-than-unanimous ratification rules. While this section points out the challenges this option raises, it stresses that Europe faces a defining moment—and emphasizes how consequential this will be for the future of the EU. Section 5 concludes.

2. Plans for the Conference

The proposal in favour of a Conference on the Future of Europe is relatively recent. Before the European Parliament (EP) elections—at a moment of profound restructuring of the party system, with a strong polarization between pro- and anti-European political forces—President Macron launched the idea: drawing from the French experience of citizens' conventions,[3] he proposed to renew the EU by putting fair and square the issue of constitutional reforms as a way to unite, strengthen, and democratize the EU and make it a sovereign power in an ever more uncertain world[4]—as he had envisioned before.[5] After the EP elections—in light of the positive result of pro-European forces, as explained in Chapter 3—the initiative was taken on board by the EU institutions, which started preparations to launch the project in 2020. In fact, while the Covid-19 pandemic delayed the originally envisioned timeframe to start the Conference on the Future of Europe, it also made it more necessary than ever—and a new momentum for this enterprise seems to have taken place with the health crisis.

2.1 Pre-Covid-19

A first strong position in favour of the Conference on the Future of Europe was taken jointly in November 2019 by France and Germany. Specifically, building on their special relationship enshrined in the Treaty of Aachen of 22 January 2019, France and Germany put forward a joint non-paper on the Conference on the Future of Europe, outlining key guidelines on

---

[3] See also French Assemblée Nationale, Commission des Affaires Européennes, Rapport d'information sur les conventions démocratique de refondation de l'Europe, N° 482, 7 December 2017.

[4] Macron (n 1).

[5] French President Emmanuel Macron, speech at Université La Sorbonne, 26 September 2017.

the project.[6] In this document, France and Germany indicated their be-lief that 'a Conference on the Future of Europe is prompt and necessary'[7] and clarified that it 'should address all issues at stake to guide the future of Europe with a view to make the EU more united and sovereign'.[8] In terms of scope, as the Franco-German proposal clarified, 'the Conference should focus on policies and identify ... the main reforms to implement as a matter of priority, setting out the types of changes to be made (legal—incl. possible treaty change ...)'.[9] Moreover, the Franco-German proposal indicated that: 'Institutional issues could also be tackled as a cross-cutting issue, to promote democracy and European values and to ensure a more efficient functioning of the Union and its Institutions.'[10] In terms of struc-ture, the Franco-German proposal indicated that the 'Conference needs to involve all three EU institutions' on the basis of an inter-institutional mandate to be agreed in early 2020.[11] Moreover, the Franco-German proposal suggested that the 'Conference could be chaired by a senior European personality', to be advised by 'a small Steering Group, con-sisting of representatives of the EU institutions, Member States, experts/civil society'.[12] Finally, in terms of scenarios, the Franco-German pro-posal stated that the Conference should work in phases—tackling insti-tutional issues first, and conclude during the French presidency of the Council in spring 2022 with final 'recommendations [to] be presented to the [European Council] for debate and implementation'.[13]

The proposal in favour of a Conference on the Future of Europe was fully taken on board by the new European Commission President Ursula von der Leyen.[14] As she pointed out when explaining her polit-ical guidelines for the 2019–2024 term before the EP on 16 July 2019, the Conference on the Future of Europe would represent 'a new push for

---

[6] See Franco-German non-paper on key questions and guidelines: Conference on the Future of Europe, 25 November 2019.

[7] Ibid 1.

[8] Ibid.

[9] Ibid.

[10] Ibid.

[11] Ibid.

[12] Ibid.

[13] Ibid 2.

[14] European Council Conclusions, 2 July 2019, EUCO 18/19, para. 3.

European democracy'.[15] In particular, President Von der Leyen stated that: 'The Conference should bring together citizens ..., civil society and European institutions as equal partners ... [and] should be well prepared with a clear scope and clear objectives, agreed between the Parliament, the Council and the Commission'.[16] Moreover, she indicated her readiness to follow up on what is agreed, including via 'Treaty change'.[17] Subsequently, in her mission letter to the Commission Vice-President-designate for Democracy and Demography Dubravka Šuica, President Von der Leyen emphasized the importance of agreeing 'on the concept, structure, timing and scope of the Conference' and ensuring 'the follow-up on what is agreed'.[18] In fact, when speaking again in front of the EP on 27 November 2019, when the whole new Commission was subject to a consent vote,[19] President Von der Leyen mentioned once more her ambition to 'mobilise Europe's best energies from all parts of our Union, from all institutions, from all walks of life, to engage in the Conference on the future of Europe'.[20] These views were subsequently outlined in a position paper of the Commission on the Conference on the Future of Europe, released on 22 January 2020.[21]

Moreover, the proposal for a Conference on the Future of Europe was also strongly backed by the EP, which quickly started preparing its position on the matter.[22] To this end, the EP set up an ad hoc working group, representing all political parties, which in December 2019 presented to the EP Conference of Presidents a detailed document outlining the EP

---

[15] European Commission President-candidate Ursula von der Leyen, 'A Union that strives for more: My agenda for Europe. Political Guidelines for the Next European Commission 2019-2024', 16 July 2019, 19.

[16] Ibid.

[17] Ibid.

[18] European Commission President Ursula von der Leyen, Mission Letter to Dubravka Šuica, 10 September 2019, 5.

[19] See European Parliament Decision of 27 November 2019 electing the Commission, P9_TA(2019)0067.

[20] European Commission President Ursula von der Leyen, speech at the European Parliament, 27 November 2019, 14.

[21] European Commission Communication, 'Shaping the Conference on the Future of Europe', 22 January 2020, COM(2020) 27 final.

[22] See also Chair of the European Parliament Constitutional Affairs (AFCO) Committee Antonio Tajani, Letter to the European Parliament President David Sassoli, 15 October 2019 (indicating consensus that the EP should play a leading role in the Conference and reporting that AFCO as the competent Committee of the EP stands ready to start working immediately to prepare the EP's position on the matter).

views on the initiative.[23] This document was subsequently embraced by the EP plenary in a resolution adopted on 15 January 2020.[24] Here, the EP underlined how 'the number of significant crises that the Union has undergone demonstrates that reform processes are needed in multiple governance areas'[25] and therefore welcomed the Conference as an opportunity 'to increase [the EU] capacity to act and make it more democratic'.[26] In terms of structure, the EP proposed that the Conference should be based on a range of bodies, including a Conference Plenary, involving also representatives of national parliaments,[27] and a Steering Committee, consisting of representatives of the EP, the Council, and the Commission.[28] Moreover, the EP also called for the establishment of an 'Executive Coordination Board [to] be composed of the three main EU institutions under Parliament's leadership',[29] with responsibilities for the daily management of the Conference. In terms of scope, then, the EP stated that the Conference should address a 'pre-defined but non-exhaustive' list of issues, including European values, democratic and institutional aspects of the EU, and some crucial policy areas.[30] Nevertheless, the EP clarified that the Conference should 'produce concrete recommendations that will need to be addressed by the institutions',[31] and called for 'a general commitment from all participants in the Conference to ensure a proper follow-up of its outcomes',[32] including 'initiating treaty change'.[33]

The proposal in favour of a Conference on the Future of Europe was also endorsed by the European Council, which on 12 December 2019 'considered the idea of a Conference on the Future of Europe starting in 2020 and ending in 2022'[34] and asked the incoming Croatian presidency of

---

[23] European Parliament Conference on the Future of Europe, Main Outcome of the Working Group, 19 December 2019.
[24] European Parliament resolution of 15 January 2020 on the European Parliament's position on the Conference on the Future of Europe, P9_TA(2020)0010.
[25] Ibid para. B.
[26] Ibid para. 2.
[27] Ibid para. 14.
[28] Ibid para. 22.
[29] Ibid para. 24.
[30] Ibid para. 7.
[31] Ibid para. 29.
[32] Ibid para. 30.
[33] Ibid para. 31.
[34] European Council Conclusions, 12 December 2019, EUCO 28/19, para. 14.

the Council 'to work towards defining a Council position on the content, scope, composition and functioning of such conference and to engage, on this basis, with the [EP] and the Commission'.[35] The European Council also underlined that the need for the Conference to respect the inter-institutional balance, and to be 'an inclusive process, with all Member States involved equally'.[36] Moreover, while the European Council stated that 'priority should be given to implementing the [2019-2024] Strategic Agenda'[37] and that the Conference should therefore 'contribute to the developments of our policies',[38] the new European Council President Charles Michel stated that the Conference should also serve as a way to change the EU by reforming it where needed.[39] On the basis of the man-date of the European Council, the Council of the EU on 3 February 2020 also put forward a draft common position in favour of the Conference on the Future of Europe.[40] Here, the Council recognized the need for 'en-gaging in a wide reflection and debate on the challenges Europe is facing and on its long-term future'[41] and proposed the creation of a light institu-tional structure, focusing on policy priorities, with a mandate to report to the European Council by 2022.

In sum, all the EU institutions have progressively embraced the plan to establish a Conference on the Future of Europe. This reflects the ambition to start a novel process, which could tackle the EU's weaknesses and re-launch European integration. In fact, following the Franco-German non-paper, several other Member States have thrown their support behind this initiative, seeing it as the way to let the EU leap forward a decade after the adoption of the Lisbon Treaty.[42] Admittedly, there are different views concerning the institutional organization and the constitutional mandate of the Conference. While the EP and several Member States individually or jointly have pushed for the Conference to have an ambitious remit, with a clear role to revise the EU treaties, the Council and other Member

---

[35] Ibid.

[36] Ibid para. 16.

[37] Ibid para. 15.

[38] Ibid.

[39] See European Parliament press release, 'Ten Years of the Lisbon Treaty and the Charter of Fundamental Rights', 18 December 2019.

[40] See Council of the EU, 3 February 2020, Doc. 5675.

[41] Ibid para. 1.

[42] See e.g. Italy non-paper for the Conference on the Future of Europe, 14 February 2020.

States are more prudent, and would prefer the process to serve as a repetition of the citizens' dialogue the EU organized in 2017–2019.[43] For this reason, a joint resolution of the three main EU institutions is awaited to sort out these issues and set the ultimate mission of the Conference. However, Covid-19 has delayed these plans.

2.2   Post-Covid-19

In fact, the explosion of the Covid-19 pandemic disrupted the time-scale originally envisioned to launch the Conference on the Future of Europe. Because of the health crisis, the joint resolution by the three main EU institutions aimed at outlining the Conference's mission was delayed. As a result, the original plan to launch the Conference on the Future of Europe on Europe Day, 9 May 2020—the 70th anniversary of the Schuman Declaration—in Dubrovnik, Croatia, was derailed.

Nevertheless, Covid-19 has actually made the need for the Conference on the Future of Europe more pressing than ever. As the EP underlined on 17 April 2020 in a broad resolution outlining its position on the action needed at EU level to combat Covid-19 and its consequences, 'the pandemic has shown the limits of the Union's capacity to act decisively and exposed the lack of the Commission's executive and budgetary powers'.[44] As a result, the EP suggested 'proposing greater powers for the Union to act in the case of cross-border health threats';[45] it called for completing EMU, and for activating 'the general *passerelle* clause to ease the decision-making process in all matters which could help to cope with the challenges of the current health crisis'.[46] More crucially, however, the EP stressed that:

the Union must be prepared to start an in-depth reflection on how to become more effective and democratic and that the current crisis only

---

[43] European Commission, 'Citizens' dialogues and citizens' consultations: Key conclusions', 30 April 2019.
[44] European Parliament resolution of 17 April 2020 on EU coordinated action to combat the Covid-19 pandemic and its consequences, P9_TA(2020)0054, para. 69.
[45] Ibid para. 67.
[46] Ibid para. 69.

heightens the urgency thereof; believes that the planned Conference on the Future of Europe is the appropriate forum to do this; is therefore of the opinion that the Conference needs to be convened as soon as possible and that it has to come forward with clear proposals, including by engaging directly with citizens, to bring about a profound reform of the Union, making it more effective, united, democratic, sovereign and resilient.[47]

The EP's call for a prompt installation of the Conference on the Future of Europe as part of the institutional responses to Covid-19 has been echoed in recent statements made by other leading policy-makers. For example, French President Emmanuel Macron once again threw his weight behind constitutional reforms in the EU, underlying how the pandemic should break any hesitation towards an in-depth rethinking of the EU.[48] At the same time, speaking in the Bundestag, the German lower house of Parliament, ahead of a crucial European Council meeting, German Chancellor Angela Merkel emphasized the need to be open towards the option of EU treaty change.[49] Moreover, EU leaders celebrated Europe's Day on 9 May 2020, reaffirming their conviction that the Conference on the Future of Europe, which 'was only delayed due to the pandemic, will be essential in developing' ideas to make the EU more transparent and more democratic.[50]

In fact, the opportunity offered by the Conference 'to open a large democratic debate on the European project [and] its reforms' was explicitly mentioned in the opening page of the 18 May 2020 Franco-German initiative for a European recovery from the Covid-19 crisis.[51] Moreover, the Conference on the Future of Europe was also mentioned by the Commission within the framework of the new ambitious European recovery plan it unveiled on 27 May 2018. Here, the Commission underlined how the health crisis 'reflects the even more important need to strengthen and nurture our democracy' and it clarified that through 'the

---

[47] Ibid para. 72.

[48] See French President Emmanuel Macron, Interview, *Financial Times*, 17 April 2020.

[49] See German Chancellor Angela Merkel, speech at the Bundestag, 23 April 2020.

[50] See European Parliament President David Sassoli, European Council President Charles Michel and European Commission President Ursula von der Leyen, Joint Op-ed, 9 May 2020.

[51] See French-German Initiative for the European Recovery from the Coronavirus Crisis, 18 May 2020.

Conference on the Future of Europe citizens should play a leading and active part in setting our priorities and our level of ambition in building a more resilient, sustainable and fair Europe'.[52] Also, the incoming trio of German, Slovenian, and Portuguese presidencies of the Council of the EU explicitly mentioned in their draft programme the firm belief 'that the Conference on the Future of Europe should deliver concrete results for the benefits of our citizens and should contribute to the development of our policies in the medium and long term so that we can better tackle current and future challenges'.[53]

Yet, it was once again the EP that put forward the most fully articulated case for speeding up the launch of the Conference on the Future of Europe post-Covid-19.[54] In an ad hoc resolution of 18 June 2020 reaffirming its prior position on the matter, the EP underlined how 'the current COVID-19 crisis has shown to a very high cost that the EU remains an unfinished project',[55] noticed how all the EU institutions have 'stated that a Conference on the Future of Europe should be organized',[56] and therefore declared its determination 'to start the Conference as soon as possible in autumn 2020'.[57] In fact, the EP stated that '10 years after the entry into force of the Lisbon Treaty, 70 years after the Schuman Declaration and in the context of the COVID-19 pandemic, the time is ripe for a reappraisal of the Union',[58] stressed that the health crisis 'made the need to reform the European Union even more apparent',[59] and therefore unequivocally claimed that the Conference should be 'open to all possible outcomes, including legislative proposals, initiating treaty change or otherwise'[60] in order to make the EU 'more democratic, more effective and more resilient'.[61]

With the EP push, on 24 June 2020 the Council of the EU also eventually formalized its position on the Conference on the Future of Europe,

---

[52] European Commission Communication, 'Europe's moment: Repair and prepare for the next generation', 27 May 2020, COM(2020) 456 final, 15.

[53] See Council of the EU, 18-months Programme of the Council, 5 June 2020, Doc. 8086/20, 5.

[54] See European Parliament resolution of 18 June 2020 on the European Parliament's position on the Conference on the Future of Europe, P9_TA(2020)0153.

[55] Ibid para. B.

[56] Ibid para. C.

[57] Ibid para. 8.

[58] Ibid para. 1.

[59] Ibid para. 2.

[60] Ibid para. 6.

[61] Ibid para. 7.

which acknowledged how 'reflecting on the challenges the EU is facing and on its future has become all the more important following the outbreak of the Covid-19 pandemic'[62]—while also stating that '[t]he Conference does not fall within the scope of Article 48 TEU'.[63] Moreover, under the leadership of the German presidency of the Council, which started on 1st July 2020, and identified the launch of the Conference as one of its priorities, the EU institutions worked to agree on a joint resolution mandating the kick-off of the Conference.[64] The initiative has therefore increasingly gained momentum—and as is often the case with such constitutional enterprises, its outcome remains wide open. Given the shortcomings of EU governance and the exigencies of the EU's recovery described in Chapter 5, the Conference on the Future of Europe potentially represents a new model to reform the EU, akin to similar out-of-the-box initiatives of the past.

3. Precedents for the Conference

The Conference on the Future of Europe—already from its name—evokes two illustrious precedents: the Conference of Messina, on the one hand, and the Convention on the Future of Europe, on the other. Both initiatives were taken at critical times in the EU's history. Both were out-of-the-box initiatives. And both proved valuable to relaunch the project of European integration.

3.1 The Conference of Messina

The Conference of Messina—which took place in the Sicilian city from 1 to 3 June 1955—is broadly regarded as a turning point in the project of European integration. Despite the successes of the 1951 Treaty of Paris establishing the European Coal and Steel Community (ECSC), the failure

---

[62] Council of the EU, 24 June 2020, Doc. 9102/20, para. 2.
[63] Ibid para. 21.
[64] See also Secretary of State for Federal, European and International Affairs of North Rhine-Westphalia Mark Speich, 'The Conference on the Future of Europe is an Opportunity', Der (europäische) Föderalist, 28 August 2020.

of the European Defence Community—and connected to that of the European Political Community—owing to a negative vote in the French Assemblée Nationale, the lower house of Parliament, on 30 August 1954 had paralysed the European project.[65] At the initiative of Italy, however, the Ministers of Foreign Affairs of the six founding Member States congressing in Messina were able to find a way to move forward in the construction of Europe.[66] In particular, as explained in a conclusive Conference resolution,[67] the governments agreed on the substantive objectives of 'the expansion of trade and the movement of persons',[68] 'more and cheaper energy',[69] and 'the setting up of a common European market'.[70] Moreover, from a procedural point of view, they decided that 'a conference or conferences will be convened for the purpose of drafting the relevant treaties or arrangements'[71] and that 'these conferences will be prepared by a Committee of government delegates assisted by experts under the chairmanship of a leading political figure whose task it will be to co-ordinate the work to be undertaken'[72] and to draft a report to be submitted to the foreign ministers by October 1955.[73]

The intergovernmental Committee established by the Conference of Messina—which came to be known as the Spaak Committee, from the name of the Belgian Minister of Foreign Affairs chairing it—worked out in meetings held in Brussels in the summer of 1955 the details of a plan to set up a common market and an atomic energy community, which were presented in a report on 21 April 1956.[74] The Ministers of Foreign Affairs of the ESCS member states meeting in a Conference in Venice in May 1956 embraced the Spaak Report and mandated an intergovernmental

---

[65] See also Richard T. Griffith, *Europe's First Constitution. The European Political Community, 1952-1954* (The Federal Trust 2000).

[66] See Enrico Serra, 'L'Italia e la Conferenza di Messina' in Enrico Serra (ed), *Il rilancio dell'Europa e i trattati di Roma* (Giuffré 1989).

[67] Resolution adopted by the Ministers of Foreign Affairs of the Member States of the ECSC at their meeting at Messina, 3 June 1955 https://www.cvce.eu/obj/resolution_adopted_by_the_foreign_ministers_of_the_ecsc_member_states_messina_1_to_3_june_1955-en-d1086bae-0c13-4a00-8608-73c75ce54fad.html.

[68] Ibid I.A.1.

[69] Ibid I.A.2.

[70] Ibid I.B.

[71] Ibid II.1.

[72] Ibid II.2.

[73] Ibid II.4.

[74] See Raymond Bertrand, 'The European Common Market Proposal' (1956) 10 *International Organization* 559.

conference (IGC), again placed under Paul-Henri Spaak's leadership, to draft a treaty.[75] Notwithstanding the futile efforts to derail the initiative staged by the UK[76]—which had been associated with the Messina process, but had refused to engage in it fully —the diplomatic talks rapidly progressed towards the drafting of two new international agreements: the treaties establishing the European Economic Community (EEC) and the European Atomic Energy Community (Euratom), both signed in Rome on 25 March 1957. The EEC and the Euratom were instituted as separate organizations from the ECSC, but shared with the latter two institutions— namely the European Court of Justice (ECJ) and the Common Assembly (the forebear of the EP).[77] As such, the Conference of Messina was able to initiate a process which—through an innovative institutional set-up, centred on a committee of experts acting under ministerial mandate— was able to expand the purview of the ECSC and relaunch the project of European integration through new international treaties, but functionally and institutionally connected to the Treaty of Paris.

3.2 The Convention on the Future of Europe

The Convention on the Future of Europe (or European Convention), instead, took place much more recently—but also at a very critical time in the process of European integration, given the incoming EU enlargement and the hostile geo-political environment. Established by the European Council meeting in Laeken, Belgium, on 14-15 December 2001,[78] the European Convention was tasked to 'resolve three basic challenges: how to bring citizens, and primarily the young, closer to the European design and the European institutions, how to organise politics and the European political area in an enlarged Union and how to develop the Union into a

---

[75] See Anne Boerger De Smedt, 'Negotiating the Foundations of European Law, 1950–57: The Legal History of the Treaties of Paris and Rome' (2012) 21 *Contemporary European History* 339, 348.

[76] See Martin Schaad, 'Plan G – A "Counterblast"? British Policy towards the Messina Countries, 1956' (1998) 7 *Contemporary European History* 39.

[77] See Jean-Marie Palayret, 'Les décideurs français et allemands face aux questions institutionnelles dans la négociation des traités de Rome 1955–57' in Marie-Thérèse Bitsch (ed), *Le couple France-Allemagne et les institutions européennes* (Bruylant 2001), 105.

[78] European Council Presidency Conclusions, Laeken, 14–15 December 2001, Annex I: Laeken Declaration.

stabilising factor and a model in the new, multipolar world'.[79] Given the difficulties in reforming the EU experienced earlier in 2001 in the negotiations of the Treaty of Nice,[80] however, the European Council 'decided to convene a Convention composed of the main parties involved in the debate on the future of the Union'[81] and tasked it 'to consider the key issues arising for the Union's future development and try to identify the various possible responses'.[82] To this end, the European Council established an original body: the Convention—modelled on the successful experiment of the Convention that had been set up two years previously to draft a Charter of Fundamental Rights for the EU, proclaimed on 7 December 2000[83]—composed by delegates of heads of state and government together with representatives of national parliaments, the EP, and the Commission.[84] Moreover, it mandated this body to prepare a final document with recommendations that would provide a starting point for discussion in the IGC, 'which will take ultimate decisions'.[85]

As is well known, however—under the leadership of its Chairman Valéry Giscard d'Estaing, a former French President and its Vice-Chairmen Giuliano Amato, a former Italian Prime Minister and Jean-Luc Dehaene, a former Belgian Prime Minister—the Convention quickly reinterpreted its mandate, and wearing the clothes of a constitution-making body engaged in a full-blown process of rethinking the institutional organization and policy competences of the EU.[86] Following an extensive process of deliberation—which ran in Brussels for 18 months starting in March 2002, through plenary meetings and thematic working groups, steered by a praesidium—the Convention drafted a new Treaty establishing a European Constitution, replacing the previous EU treaties and codifying EU primary law into a single text with an explicit constitutional character.[87] This draft treaty, agreed by consensus, was presented

---

[79] Ibid II.
[80] See also Declaration No 23 on the future of the Union annexed to the Treaty of Nice, OJ 2001 C 80/85 (calling for 'a deeper and wider debate about the future of the European Union') .
[81] Laeken Declaration, III.
[82] Ibid.
[83] See Gráinne de Búrca, 'The Drafting of the European Union Charter of Fundamental Rights' (2015) 40 *European Law Review* 799.
[84] Laeken Declaration, III.
[85] Ibid.
[86] See Peter Norman, *The Accidental Constitution* (Eurocomment 2005).
[87] See Jean-Claude Piris, *The Constitution for Europe. A Legal Analysis* (CUP 2010).

to the European Council on 18 July 2003 and served as the basis for the subsequent IGC. Despite some adaptations which several Member States' governments required during the intergovernmental negotiations, the draft treaty prepared by the Convention was mostly embraced pari passu by the IGC, and the then 25 EU Member States thus signed the Treaty establishing a Constitution for Europe in Rome on 29 October 2004.[88] Alas, as explained in Chapter 5, this treaty encountered a ratification crisis, leading ultimately to the abandonment of the constitutional language.[89] Yet, its substance was eventually preserved via the Treaty of Lisbon.[90] As such, the European Convention—through an innovative institutional set up, with a mixed composition and a transparent deliberative process—was able to come up with a grand plan of EU reforms, which in the end allowed the process of European integration to move forward on a stronger basis for another decade.

In sum, both the Conference of Messina and the Convention on the Future of Europe represented historical turning points in the process of European integration—which serve as important precedents for the Conference on the Future of Europe. Indeed, both were out-of-the-box initiatives, which were able to change the political dynamics of inter-state bargaining through new institutional methods.[91] And both resulted in documents which profoundly influenced the development of integration, albeit in different ways.

4. Prospects for the Conference

The Conference on the Future of Europe represents potentially a major initiative to relaunch the project of European integration and reform the EU, along the lines of the historical precedents of the Conference of Messina and the Convention on the Future of Europe. To achieve its ambitious objectives, however, the Conference on the Future of Europe

---

[88] See Paul Craig, 'Constitutional Process and Reform in the EU: Nice, Laeken, the Convention and the IGC' (2004) 10 *European Public Law* 653.

[89] See European Council Presidency Conclusions, 21–22 June 2007, Annex I, para. 1.

[90] See Paul Craig, *The Lisbon Treaty: Law, Politics, and Treaty Reform* (OUP 2010).

[91] See Koen Lenaerts & Marlies Desomer, 'New Models of Constitution-Making in Europe: The Quest for Legitimacy?' (2002) 39 *Common Market Law Review* 1217.

must be directed towards treaty change as this is the main way to address the shortcomings that have emerged in the context of Europe's multiple crises, culminating with Covid-19. Nevertheless, as underlined in Chapter 5, formidable obstacles surround the recourse to the treaty amendment procedure. This is why EU Member States have increasingly resorted to inter se agreements outside the EU legal order, particularly in the field of EMU, where they have codified special rules on approval and entry into force of these new treaties overcoming the unanimity rule. As such, policy-makers involved in the Conference should seek to draw lessons from this experience, as well as from the successes and failures of prior efforts at treaty change, and consider creative options going forward—notably that of drafting a new Political Compact, with new rules on its entry into force. Clearly, the success of the Conference on the Future of Europe cannot be taken for granted and manifold challenges surround this initiative—but there is no doubt that the EU faces a defining moment.

4.1 The Option of a Political Compact

The analysis of the legal rules and political options for treaty reform in the EU provides a crucial insight for policy-makers engaged in the nascent Conference on the Future of Europe. This is the awareness that the rules on the entry into force of any reform treaty resulting from the Conference will have a major impact on the success of the initiative. Because of the veto-points embedded in Article 48 TEU, any major reform plan that may emerge from the Conference on the Future of Europe risks foundering on the rocks of the unanimity requirement. After all, this is precisely the reason why EU Member States have opted not to use the standard EU amendment procedure to respond to the euro-crisis, but have instead acted outside the EU legal framework, adopting new intergovernmental treaties which did not require approval by all the Member States to enter into force. The precedents set by the Fiscal Compact,[92] the treaty

---

[92] Treaty on Stability, Coordination and Governance in the Economic and Monetary Union, 2 March 2012 http://www.eurozone.europa.eu/media/304649/st00tscg26_en12.pdf.

establishing the European Stability Mechanism (ESM)[93] and the inter-governmental agreement on the Single Resolution Fund (SRF),[94] however, offer a roadmap that institutional players in the Conference on the Future of Europe should use. To avoid the fate of the Treaty establishing the European Constitution—which was drafted by consensus in the European Convention, but sunk by two negative national referenda—the Conference on the Future of Europe could channel the outcome of its process into a new treaty with new rules on the entry into force of the treaty itself, which do away with the unanimity requirement and thus change the dynamics of the ratification game in the 27 Member States.

Specifically, the Conference on the Future of Europe could propose the drafting of a new treaty—call it a Political Compact. This would be an international agreement, functionally and institutionally connected to the EU, just like the EMU-related treaties adopted in the aftermath of the euro-crisis. The Political Compact would need to address many of the shortcomings in the EU's governance system that have been exposed by recent crises—examined in Chapter 4—and deal with the EU's effectiveness and legitimacy deficits—analysed in Chapter 5. However—leaving aside here what the content of this treaty could be, which should be precisely the duty of the Conference on the Future of Europe—the Political Compact should set new rules on its entry into force, which do away with the unanimity requirement. In particular, the Political Compact could foresee its entry into force when ratified by a super-majority of for example 19 Member States, which corresponds to about three-quarters of the EU Member States. Just like the Fiscal Compact—and contrary to the ESM Treaty and the SRF Agreement—the ratification of each Member State would count the same, consistent with the principle of the international equality of states. But contrary to the Fiscal Compact, both Eurozone and non-Eurozone Member States would weigh towards ratification. Moreover—contrary to prior academic proposals to overcome unanimity in treaty amendments[95]—the treaty would not apply to the

[93] See Treaty Establishing the European Stability Mechanism, 2 February 2012 http://www.european-council.europa.eu/media/582311/05-tesm2.en12.pdf.

[94] See Agreement on the transfer and mutualisation of contributions to the Single Resolution Fund, 21 May 2014 http://register.consilium.europa.eu/doc/srv?l=EN&f=ST%208457%20 2014%20INIT.

[95] See Hervé Bribosia et al, 'Revising the European Treaties: A Plea in Favour of Abolishing the Veto', Notre Europe Policy Paper No 37/2009.

non-ratifying states, guaranteeing them the free choice of whether or not to join the Political Compact, with all the consequences that follow.

The proposal put forward here resembles the one advanced at the time of the Convention by the Commission in its Penelope project, mentioned in Chapter 5.[96] Nevertheless, it differs from it in one essential way. The Penelope project proposal sought to amend the EU treaties with a procedure that by its own admission broke the rules of Article 48 TEU itself. On the contrary, the proposal advanced here would be consistent with the treaties, as it would not surreptitiously amend Article 48 TEU, but rather set a new ratification rule for a new, inter se treaty. In fact, by being drafted as a separate inter-state agreement—and provided this would not introduce any measure explicitly inconsistent with EU law—the Political Compact could meet the criteria of legality set by the ECJ in *Pringle* when reviewing the ESM treaty.[97] Moreover, while the overcoming of the unanimity rule in the ratification process was unheard of, and revolutionary, in 2002, today the practice has now become real, and indeed quite ordinary: the Fiscal Compact, the ESM Treaty, and the SRF Agreement represent important precedents to follow.

At the same time, however, the option to conclude a separate Political Compact treaty as the outcome of the Conference would mitigate many of the criticisms that have been raised during the negotiations of the EMU intergovernmental agreements. In fact, the processes of drafting the Fiscal Compact, the ESM Treaty, and the SRF Agreement were purely diplomatic and secretive negotiations, which left out the EP, save for the pro-forma involvement of the Chairman of the EP Economic and Monetary Affairs (ECON) Committee.[98] On the contrary, the Conference on the Future of Europe would be a much more open, transparent, and participatory process—and with full input from, and involvement by, the EP, which will in fact play a leading role in the steering of the Conference, and influencing its output. Therefore, one could expect the Conference to steer away from the perils of intergovernmental decision-making,

---

[96] See European Commission, Feasibility Study: Contribution to a Preliminary Draft Constitution of the European Union, 4 December 2002 https://www.europarl.europa.eu/meetdocs/committees/afco/20021217/const051202_en.pdf.

[97] See Case C-370/12 *Pringle*, ECLI:EU:C:2012:756.

[98] See Valentin Kreilinger, 'The making of a new treaty: six rounds of political bargaining', Notre Europe Policy Brief No 32/2012.

and that its output would instead resemble the features of the Treaty establishing the European Constitution produced by the democratic deliberations of the European Convention.

For these reasons, it seems likely that the Political Compact would withstand any judicial review of its EU legality. Indeed, as previously mentioned, the ECJ is competent to review that inter se agreements concluded outside the EU treaties are compatible with EU law.[99] Yet, in *Pringle* the ECJ found that the ESM Treaty passed the test, and simultaneously clarified that Member States are free to expand the powers of the EU institutions as long as this extra grant of authority does not alter their essential functions. Moreover, in *Wightman* the ECJ ruled that the EU treaties' aim to create 'an ever closer union among the peoples of Europe' has clear legal consequences (in that case, the possibility for a Member State to revoke its notification of the intention to withdraw from the EU).[100] By these standards, it seems that a Political Compact making the EU more effective and democratic would certainly be consistent with the guidelines set by the ECJ. In fact, if the outcome of the Conference on the Future of Europe were to be subject to ECJ review, it seems plausible to claim that it could be looked at even more approvingly than the ESM treaty, which was the result of a purely intergovernmental process.[101] And at the same time, if the Political Compact could represent the way to allow the project of EU integration to move forward, on a more solid basis between those who want it, the initiative would be consistent with the treaties' aim to create 'an ever closer union among the peoples of Europe'.

In fact, from a constitutional point of view, there is a major precedent for what is suggested here—namely the adoption of the oldest and most revered basic law in the world: the Constitution of the United States (US). While after the War of Independence in 1781 the 13 North American colonies had come together and established a union under the Articles of Confederation, this first constitution proved unable to serve

---

[99] See Chapter 5, section 4.1.

[100] See Case C-621/18 *Wightman*, ECLI:EU:C:2018:999 (holding that the notification of Article 50 TEU can be revoked as a consequence of the commitment by Member States enshrined in the treaties to achieve ever closer union).

[101] See also Federico Fabbrini, 'The Euro-Crisis and the Courts' (2014) 32 *Berkeley Journal of International Law* 64.

the interests of the nascent US well.[102] As a result, in 1787, a convention of states' delegates was called in Philadelphia to propose amendments to the Articles.[103] However, this Convention reinterpreted its mandate and drafted a brand new document: the Constitution of the US.[104] Crucially, however, the framers set into the Constitution itself the rule that ratification by nine (out of 13) states would suffice for its entry into force.[105] As explained by Michael Klarman, this was technically a breach of the Articles of Confederation,[106] which required unanimous consent by the 13 states to amend the Articles themselves.[107] However, by replacing the Articles' unanimity requirement with a super-majority one for the entry into force of the new Constitution—and by requiring this to be approved by special states' ratifying conventions set up exclusively for this task—the framers were able to circumvent the opposition of some states, which otherwise would have doomed the whole constitutional endeavour.[108]

Needless to say, if the Conference on the Future of Europe were to foresee a new ratification rule for the entry into force of a treaty resulting from its works, this could sanction the path towards a decoupling of the EU.[109] Indeed, Member States which did not ratify the Political Compact would be left out from the new architecture of integration. Nevertheless, one should not underestimate the pressuring effect that this would have on states which are prima facie reluctant to ratify a treaty—a dynamic which as mentioned was visible in Ireland where the Fiscal Compact was approved in a referendum in 2012. As Carlos Closa has explained, the introduction of less than unanimous treaty entry-into-force rules profoundly changes the ratification game and creates strong incentives for the hold-outs to join the treaty once this has reached the necessary number of ratifications to enter into force.[110] Moreover, one must

---

[102] See Douglas Smith, 'An Analysis of Two Federal Structures: the Articles of Confederation and the Constitution' (1997) 34 *San Diego Law Review* 249.

[103] See Gordon Wood, *The Creation of the American Republic: 1776-1787* (Norton 1993).

[104] See Max Farrand, *Records of the Federal Convention, Volume 1* (Yale University Press 1911).

[105] See Art. VII, US Constitution.

[106] Michael Klarman, *The Framers' Coup: The Making of the United States Constitution* (OUP 2016).

[107] See Art. XIII, Articles of Confederation.

[108] See also Bruce Ackerman and Neal Katyal, 'Our Unconventional Founding' (1995) 62 *University of Chicago Law Review* 475 (explaining that the last state—Rhode Island—only ratified the US Constitution in 1790, two years after it had already entered into force for the other states, and when a new federal government was already in place).

[109] See Sergio Fabbrini, *Europe's Future: Decoupling and Reforming* (CUP 2019).

[110] See also Carlos Closa, *The Politics of Ratification of EU Treaties* (Routledge 2013).

acknowledge that the process of EU differentiation has been going on for a while—particularly in the context of the Eurozone, which has increasingly acquired features of its own.[111] And the recent crises that the EU has weathered have further divided—rather than united—the EU, as shown in Chapter 4. For this reason, a Political Compact could be seen as a positive step to relaunch European integration among the Member States that are willing to build a strong and sovereign political union, circumventing the opposition that could come for instance from countries which are increasingly at odds with the EU's founding principles and values.[112]

4.2 The Challenge of a Defining Moment

The Conference on the Future of Europe has the potential to be a turning point for the EU and, as I have claimed in a study commissioned by the EP Constitutional Affairs (AFCO) Committee, the option to draft a Political Compact, with new rules on its entry into force, represents the possible avenue for further political integration in Europe.[113] Nevertheless, it is clear that the success of this initiative cannot be taken for granted. Therefore, the future of the EU27 remains uncertain and unsettled, with several prospects ahead. On the one hand, as pointed out in Chapter 4, the competing visions on the *finalité* of Europe—with the clash between a polity, a market, and an autocracy *Weltanschauung* of integration—complicate further the reform prospects. On the other hand, there is a serious risk of complacency which may hamper the momentum going forward. Indeed, it is often argued that path-dependency is a defining feature of the EU.[114] As a consequence, leading voices in politics as well as in academia have discarded as idealistic the scenario of grand reform for the EU, arguing instead that the EU ultimately always manages to carry on from one crisis to the next—and that muddling through, right or wrong, is the natural way to do business.[115]

---

[111] See Jean-Claude Piris, *The Future of Europe: Towards a Two-Speed EU?* (CUP 2011).

[112] See Chapter 4, section 2.3.

[113] See Federico Fabbrini, 'Possible Avenues for Further Political Integration in Europe', study commissioned by the European Parliament Constitutional Affairs Committee, May 2020.

[114] See Paul Pierson, 'The Path to European Integration: A Historical Institutionalist Analysis' (1996) 29 *Comparative Political Studies* 123.

[115] See Andy Moravcsik, 'Europe's Ugly Future: Muddling Through Austerity' (2016) 95 *Foreign Affairs* 139.

However, if Brexit shows anything, it is precisely that the ability of the EU to muddle through has limits. Even discounting the UK's idiosyncratic approach to European integration, there is no doubt that its withdrawal from the EU sounded an alarm bell.[116] As many have emphasized, the EU is in disequilibrium,[117] and the status quo is not sustainable in the long term.[118] After the Brexit referendum, some had worried that the EU project may be about to unravel—but the embarrassing difficulties faced by the UK in leaving the EU later reassured many that no other Member State would attempt to trigger Article 50 TEU.[119] And yet, withdrawal is just one among several ways in which disintegration may actually occur.[120] In fact, a slower form of cancerous erosion of the union is also possible. After all, in families—like in federations—a union relies on the assumption that we 'sink or swim together'[121]—and if this moral bond withers, there is little that laws can do to replace it.[122]

Hence, the EU is indeed facing a defining moment. From this point of view, therefore, it will be crucial for those Member States' governments that have so far maintained a constructive ambiguity on their visions of integration to take a firm stance on what Europe they want—effectively choosing between the models of 'polity', 'market', and 'autocracy' outlined in Chapter 4. This is particularly true for Germany, which is the largest and wealthiest EU Member State. Whereas historically the German government had supported a polity vision of Europe, since the reunification

---

[116] See Hannes Hofmeister (ed), *The End of the Ever Closer Union?* (Nomos 2018).

[117] See Dermot Hodson and Uwe Puetter, 'The European Union in disequilibrium' (2019) 26 *Journal of European Public Policy* 1153.

[118] See Ronan McCrea, 'Forward or Back: The Future of European Integration and the Impossibility of the Status Quo' (2017) 23 *European Law Journal* 66.

[119] See Marlene Wind, 'Brexit and Euroskepticism: Will "Leaving Europe" be Emulated Elsewhere?' in Federico Fabbrini (ed), *The Law & Politics of Brexit* (OUP 2017), 221.

[120] See Mark Dawson, 'Coping with Exit, Evasion, and Subversion in EU Law' (2020) 21 *German Law Journal* 51.

[121] See US Supreme Court, *Edwards v. California*, 314 U.S. 160, 174 (1941) (defining the US as 'framed under the dominion of a political philosophy less parochial in range. It was framed upon the theory that the peoples of the several States must sink or swim together, and that, in the long run, prosperity and salvation are in union, and not division').

[122] But see Joined Cases C-715/17, C-718/17 and C-719/17 *Commission v Hungary, Poland and the Czech Republic*, Opinion of AG Sharpston, ECLI:EU:C:2019:917, para. 255 (saying that Member States should not sabotage the union, recalling 'an old story from the Jewish tradition that deserves wider circulation. A group of men are travelling together in a boat. Suddenly, one of them takes out an auger and starts to bore a hole in the hull beneath himself. His companions remonstrate with him. "Why are you doing that?" they cry. "What are you complaining about?" says he. "Am I not drilling the hole under my own seat?" "Yes," they reply, "but the water will come in and flood the boat for all of us"').

its position has been blurred. Under the leadership of Chancellor Angela Merkel—and under the noxious influence of domestic institutions like its Constitutional Court, the Bundesverfassungsgericht (BVerfG)—the German government dragged its feet and failed convincingly to answer French President Macron's call to relaunch the EU's political project jointly. Despite signing the Meseberg Declaration in June 2018,[123] the German government resisted solving the euro-crisis' legacy by completing EMU,[124] and—as noted in Chapter 3—initially lobbied for a smaller MFF 2021–2027. Moreover, while taking bold measures to deal with the migration crisis, it pushed for further EU enlargements, and has been cautiously silent regarding the rule of law backsliding in Hungary—perhaps because Prime Minister Viktor Orbán's party is a member of the European People's Party, to which Chancellor Merkel's Christian Democrats also belong.[125]

However, in the second semester of 2020 Germany took over the presidency of the Council of the EU—which gives it a unique opportunity to bring leadership and energy into the effort to think strategically about the future of Europe, and reform the EU accordingly. Moreover, in its latest policy choices, the German government has more boldly defended the EU as a political project—as voiced by many influential German intellectuals.[126] For example, together with France the German government backed an ambitious recovery fund for the post-Covid-19 reconstruction,[127] which, as has been pointed out, represented a change of paradigm, as Germany for the first time leaned towards the creation of common EU debt.[128] Moreover, the German government also endorsed with France an initiative to create an EU data infrastructure—Gaia-X,[129]

---

[123] Franco-German Declaration, Meseberg, 19 June 2018.

[124] See Wade Jacoby, 'Surplus Germany' (2020) 29 *German Politics* 498.

[125] See also Dan Kelemen, 'Europe's Other Democratic Deficit: National Authoritarianism in Europe's Democratic Union' (2017) 52 *Government & Opposition* 211.

[126] See Joschka Fischer & Jürgen Habermas, 'Nous appelons la Commission européenne à créer un fonds corona pour aider les Etats membres', Op-ed, *Le Monde*, 3 April 2020 (calling on Germany to abandon its reticence and take a firm stance in favour of European solidarity in responding to Covid-19).

[127] See French-German Initiative for the European Recovery from the Coronavirus Crisis, 18 May 2020.

[128] See also German Finance Minister Olaf Scholz, Interview, *Die Zeit*, 19 May 2020.

[129] See Ministère de l'Economie et des Finance, communique de presse conjoint, 'Sous l'impulsion de l'Allemagne et la France, l'Europe fait un premier pas vers une infrastructure de données', 4 June 2020, n° 2186.

which reflects a shared ambition to endow the EU with greater digital sovereignty.[130]

The more explicit German government's stance in favour of further political integration in the EU creates a window of opportunity for the Conference on the Future of Europe, as the German presidency could set in motion the process and put it on a track towards success—by the time of the French presidency of the Council of the EU in 2020. No doubt, resistance is likely to be met. But Germany's ability to deal with this—as well as the positions it will take in crafting Europe's responses to the catastrophic Covid-19 pandemic—will go a long way in answering the question of whether the EU will further integrate or disintegrate in the future.

5. Conclusion

This chapter has analysed the EU beyond Brexit—discussing the establishment of the Conference on the Future of Europe. Originally envisioned by French President Macron, and now endorsed by all EU institutions and the other Member States, the Conference has major potentials. It may be a new model to reform the EU, addressing the substantive and institutional weaknesses exposed by old and new crises. And it can be a ground-breaking initiative to relaunch European integration—channelling towards concrete action the debate on the future of Europe that started since the Brexit referendum. In fact, while Covid-19 delayed the original plan for the Conference's launch, it has also made it more necessary than ever—showing that the EU does not need reform for the sake of reform itself, but rather to address real and present shortcomings in its constitutional architecture. As such, the Conference on the Future of Europe can potentially be an innovative, out-of-the-box enterprise to renew the EU, along the lines of illustrious precedents such as the Conference of Messina and the Convention on the Future of Europe.

However, as the Conference on the Future of Europe takes off and figures out its mission, it is important it bears in mind the constraints of treaty reform. Article 48 TEU foresees a cumbersome process of treaty

---

[130] See also Federico Fabbrini et al (eds), *Data Protection Beyond Borders* (Hart Publishing 2021).

amendment. This is why Member States have increasingly resorted to inter se agreements outside the EU legal order—notably to reform EMU. In light of this experience, this chapter has suggested that architects of the Conference on the Future of Europe should consider drafting a Political Compact, i.e. a separate treaty subject to new ratification rules which do away with the requirement of unanimous approval by all Member States. While this would remove the risks of the Conference's outcome foundering on the cliffs of state vetoes in the ratification process, and therefore avoid the disappointments of predecessors like the European Constitution, there is no doubt that this option raises novel challenges— even leaving aside what the content of the Political Compact should be. Yet, the EU faces a defining moment, and the fate of the Conference will shape the future of European integration going forward.

7

Conclusion

This book has analysed Brexit and the future of the European Union (EU), making the case for constitutional reforms. The withdrawal of the United Kingdom (UK) from the EU is a momentous event, which represents a watershed in the history of European integration. For the first time a Member State decided to leave the EU, bringing to an end 60 years of uninterrupted widening and deepening of the EU, and shattering the narrative of the EU's irreversibility. To blame this event simply on the UK's idiosyncratic approach to European integration is an underestimation of the deep centrifugal dynamics at play in the EU. And to minimize Brexit, carrying on with business as usual is a failure to appreciate the significance of this development. Brexit is a big deal. As French President Emmanuel Macron put it on an open letter written to the British people on 1 February 2020, the first day after the UK's exit, '[t]his departure has to be a shock, because there is nothing trivial about it. We must understand the reasons for it and learn lessons from it'.[1]

While it is a matter of opinion whether the departure of the UK represents a tragic development for the EU, or rather an opportunity for further integration,[2] there is no doubt that Brexit had pervasive consequences for the EU—and so it continues to be. As recently as on 19 June 2020—almost six months after the formal withdrawal of the UK from the EU on 31 January 2020—Brexit was still on the European Council agenda:[3] in a summit which was primarily meant to facilitate a preliminary negotiation among heads of state and government on the European Commission's grand strategy for a post-pandemic recovery plan,[4] leaders

---

[1] French President Emmanuel Macron, Letter, 1 February 2020, https://www.elysee.fr/en/emmanuel-macron/2020/02/01/a-letter-from-emmanuel-macron-to-the-british-people.

[2] See 'The EU's recovery fund is a benefit of Brexit', *The Economist*, 30 May 2020 (arguing that the UK's withdrawal from the EU facilitated the Commission proposal in favour of a recovery plan, by removing the UK veto).

[3] See European Council President Charles Michel, remarks, 19 June 2020, 415/20.

[4] See European Commission Communication, 'Europe's moment: Repair and prepare for the Next Generation', 27 May 2020, COM(2020) 456 final.

Brexit and the Future of the European Union. Federico Fabbrini, Oxford University Press (2020). © Federico Fabbrini. DOI: 10.1093/oso/9780198871262.003.0007

discussed the high-level meeting that the EU had had four days before with UK Prime Minister Boris Johnson to take stock of the negotiations on the future framework of EU–UK relations,[5] which will shape the relations between the EU27 and the UK after the end of the Brexit transition period.

As such, Brexit is an exceptional historical development that must be studied for the lasting consequences it has on the EU—but also taken as a warning call to start a constitutional reform process in the EU. In fact, reforms are not needed for the sake of reform itself: rather, they are much needed to make the EU more united, sovereign, and democratic, and the UK's withdrawal from the EU should be seen as removing any refrain to the contrary. As the first visible instance of disintegration in the fabric of the EU, Brexit proves that there can no longer be complacency among national and EU leaders on the status quo: the current EU constitutional settlement is unsustainable, and reforms are overdue—not only to tackle the legacy issues of the UK's withdrawal, but also to improve the EU's effectiveness and legitimacy, so as to make it ready to tackle the exigencies of the post-Covid-19 recovery, and fit to address the geo-political challenges of a new era.[6]

This book has used Brexit as a prism to shed light on the EU and its future. While the EU27 responded in a united fashion to the UK's decision to leave the EU, and stuck together during the withdrawal negotiations, Brexit caused a set of transitional issues of the EU's funding and functioning. Moreover, besides Brexit the EU27 faced a plurality of crises—from the euro-crisis, to the migration crisis and the rule of law crisis—which significantly tested their unity, bringing to the surface conflicting visions of integration. In fact, the challenges for the EU and its Member States have increased after Brexit, as a result of the explosion of Covid-19, a global pandemic with catastrophic human and socio-economic costs. Beyond Brexit, therefore, it is high time for the EU to move its reflection process from rhetoric to reality, and the launch of the Conference on the Future of Europe is a very welcome step in this direction.

---

[5] See EU-UK Statement following the High Level Meeting, 15 June 2020, STATEMENT/20/1067.
[6] See also European Commission President Ursula von der Leyen, statement, 10 September 2019.

The Conference on the Future of Europe—an idea originally put forward by French President Emmanuel Macron in March 2019 in an open letter addressed to all European citizens (written in the 22 official languages of the EU) *pour une renaissance européenne*,[7] and subsequently endorsed by all EU institutions[8]—has the potential to be a groundbreaking initiative to address the shortcomings in the EU's system of governance, patently exposed by the series of recent crises. Otherwise, the need to reform the EU to increase its effectiveness and legitimacy is further compounded by the exigencies of the post-Covid-19 recovery, which by deploying unprecedented fiscal measures call to back up these structural changes with adequate constitutional adjustments. Hence, while Covid-19 has delayed the original timeframe for the Conference's launch, it has also made it more urgent than ever.

However, if the Conference on the Future of Europe wants to succeed in its ambitious goal, it must deal with the challenges of treaty change in the EU. The formal treaty amendment procedure, in fact, creates powerful obstacles to reform—owing to the need of unanimous approval and ratification by all Member States. Yet, it is precisely to overcome the problem of the veto that Member States have increasingly resorted—notably in the context of the euro-crisis—to intergovernmental agreements outside the EU legal order. In these new inter se treaties, states have introduced new rules on the treaties' entry into force, which do away with the unanimity rule. This constitutes an important precedent.

As this book has suggested, the Conference on the Future of Europe should reflect about channelling its output into a new, separate treaty—call it a Political Compact—with less than unanimous rules on its entry into force. By doing so, the Conference on the Future of Europe could follow in the footsteps of some illustrious precedents, notably the Conference of Messina and the Convention on the Future of Europe, and serve as an out-of-the-box initiative to renew the EU. Certainly, even

<hr />

[7] French President Emmanuel Macron, Letter, 4 March 2019 https://www.elysee.fr/es/emmanuel-macron/2019/03/04/pour-une-renaissance-europeenne.fr.

[8] See European Parliament resolution of 15 January 2020 on the European Parliament's position on the Conference on the Future of Europe, P9_TA(2020)0010; European Commission Communication, 'Shaping the Conference on the Future of Europe', 22 January 2020, COM(2020) 27 final; European Parliament resolution of 18 June 2020 on the European Parliament's position on the Conference on the Future of Europe, P9_TA(2020)0153; and Council of the EU, 24 June 2020, Doc. 9102/20.

leaving aside its content, which would be for the Conference to deliberate on, the option of drafting a Political Compact raises questions. However, by overcoming the veto points embedded in the treaty amendment process, this represents a possible avenue towards further political integration in Europe, which is preferable to the risk of paralysis.

Admittedly, the EU remains unsettled, and its prospects uncertain. Indeed, three alternative visions on what integration is and ought to be are increasingly competing with each other: a first that sees the EU as a polity, which requires solidarity and a communion of efforts towards a shared destiny; a second that sees the EU as a market, designed to enhance wealth through commerce, but with as limited redistribution as possible; and a third which instead sees the EU as a vehicle to entrench state autocracy, based on national identity and sovereignty claims, but with crucial transnational financial support. Reconciling these *Weltanschauungen* will not be easy. However as Brexit has proved, the current constitutional settlement is wanting, and the EU's legitimacy and effectiveness must be improved to contain further centrifugal pressures.

From this point of view, the Conference on the Future of Europe can be an innovative endeavour to relaunch European integration. And the option to draft a new Political Compact for a more democratic and effective union can be an inventive solution to renew the EU despite political disagreements on its *finalité*. After all, as architecture scholar Sebastiano Fabbrini has pointed out, 'the process of European integration is constantly described in architectural terms'[9]—and the EU, as any construction site, requires constant restructuring. While the Conference on the Future of Europe faces the challenges of a defining moment, therefore, the EU must react to Brexit, reform itself, and march towards a 'more perfect Union'.[10]

---

[9] See Sebastiano Fabbrini, 'Whatever Happened to Supranational Architecture?' (2021) 7 *Ardeth*.

[10] Preamble, US Constitution.

Index

For the benefit of digital users, indexed terms that span two pages (e.g., 52–53) may, on occasion, appear on only one of those pages.

Tables are indicated by *t* following the page number